You Are Worth It

You Are Worth It

Feel comfortable communicating your fees & achieve the income your services deserve

Ashley Latter

authorHOUSE®

AuthorHouse™ UK Ltd.
1663 Liberty Drive
Bloomington, IN 47403 USA
www.authorhouse.co.uk
Phone: 0800.197.4150

Published by AuthorHouse   01/07/2014

ISBN: 978-1-4918-8930-5 (sc)
ISBN: 978-1-4918-8931-2 (e)

Printed in the United States of America by BookMasters, Inc
Ashland OH
April 2015

Contents

Testimonials

In July 2013, I eventually attended the two-day 'Ethical Sales and Communication' programme presented by Ashley Latter in Cork.

The programme had been recommended to me a year previously in Dublin by Yvonne from Henry Schein. I balked at the fee then but can now say it was one of the two best investments I've made in my practice in twenty-nine years of dentistry.

The return on investment has been phenomenal. In the four weeks after taking the course, I scheduled and took impressions for fifteen six-month smile cases. We have averaged 1.5 cases a week since I attended the course. I put this down to the changes Ashley encouraged and taught us to make in our case presentations.

I strongly urge anyone considering the course to get on it ASAP. It affects every area of your practice positively. You will learn so much more than presenting cases.

Regards,
John Seward

*   *   *

Before taking the course, I struggled with discussing treatments with patients, in particular where money was involved. After taking the course, wow! My practicing life has changed completely. In only eight weeks I have managed to deliver the treatments I have been trained to do! And my word-of-mouth referrals have rocketed as well in a short time. The course has also helped with my overall confidence, both with patients and with colleagues and peers.

I cannot thank you enough, Ashley. You have given me a new way of thinking, which is that I can achieve anything I set out to do.

For anyone who is unsure, please just do the course. You will not believe how much this will change your practicing life/career. It certainly has for me, and I would recommend it to any dentists who want to progress their careers and deliver the best for their patients.

Sanaa Kader

*　　*　　*

We knew we had to do something to improve our treatment plan acceptance rate. I looked at a number of options, but after seeing your presentation at this year's dentistry show, I finally found the solution.

I. The changes in both of us have been incredible and the impact on the business amazing. We have a systemised sales approach and a toolkit that we draw upon to convert our treatment plans. Within a week of attending your course, our uptake of treatment increased significantly, and we continue to build on this.

I had high expectations in attending your course, and I am happy to say you far exceeded them. Attending it was undoubtedly the best business decision we have made this year. Attending it together, which gave us a joined-up approach, was the second best decision. My only regret is that we didn't involve the whole team, but they are enjoying reading your book, *Don't Wait for the Tooth Fairy*. We will be investing in some in-house training in the very near future.

My advice to anyone considering attending your course is to stop wasting time and book today. They too will be amazed by the results.

Regards,

Lesley Morgan Barlow

Acknowledgements

To the Latter girls Graziella, Enrica and Martina—love you so much x

To my Mum and Dad—none of this could happen without you. Your guidance and affection has meant so much to me.

To Alistair Mann for helping me put this book together.

To Lissa for holding the fort and providing World Class Service to our clients

To all my clients who have taken my presentations and courses over the last 22 years. What an incredible journey.

Foreword by Nadim Majid

It was a Holiday Inn, I think, in Manchester on a Saturday. I had just listened to an excellent lecture on composites and materials. The next presentation was on marketing and sales. I was thinking about going home early; it had been a long day, and I had a busy evening ahead. I don't know what made me stay, although I am glad I did. For the next forty minutes I was introduced to Ashley Latter, a very entertaining and educational speaker.

The thing that stood out for me more than any other was one PowerPoint slide about getting out of your comfort zone to continue to push yourself, as all the rewards, all the gifts, lie outside of the comfort zones that we build around us.

Towards the end of the presentation Ashley shared his personal story of how he pushed himself from a struggling salesman to a globally successful one and then left that market completely to coach dentists on sales and marketing.

Ashley is someone who is authentic to the message he teaches. He continues to push himself out of his own comfort zone because ultimately these lessons are passed on to the clients he serves and help them to succeed.

Price and pricing strategy are subjects highly important to any business; they can make or break a business. Ashley has always taught his clients to ethically and confidently price their products and services according to what they deserve and what they are worth. There are very few books on this subject, let alone specialised texts for the dental field. Knowing Ashley and the amount of time and effort he dedicates to all endeavours, I can guarantee that long days and night have been poured into this book. I am confident it will serve all who read and implement what is in these pages.

So if you have lived in your comfort zone for too long and see your goals and dreams just out of reach, take the first step towards achieving more by reading on.

Dr Nadim Majid

Foreword by Michael Cahill

I have had the pleasure of knowing Ashley for over fifteen years now, and have taken many of his excellent courses in that time. Initially I attended on my own, but it soon became obvious that having the whole team learn along with me would be key to implementing the principles Ashley coaches.

I therefore made a significant investment and engaged Ashley to train my practice team for a whole year! I can honestly say that what we all learned during that time has become a core part of our ethos at the practice, and has been instrumental in the development of the business. Since then, every new team member has been trained by Ashley.

This book, the second of Ashley's forays into business writing, is an invaluable tool for the whole of the dental team. Unfortunately we are not taught how to develop and run a business at dental school, and many of us will have made a whole range of mistakes in evolving our practices. Ashley's clear, concise, and easy-to-read book will help to minimise those mistakes. It is packed with tips, ideas, and practical suggestions for improving any business, and should be required reading for all dentists, whether newly qualified or with years of experience.

Read this book now. You're definitely worth it!

Dr Michael Cahill

Introduction: Why I wrote this book

Over the last twenty years, I have personally trained and coached almost seven thousand dentists via my two-day 'Ethical Sales and Communication' programme. I have visited hundreds of practices, spent hours socialising with dentists, and presented to thousands of them and their teams all over the world. That insight and those invaluable experiences have now led me to issue this bold statement: *I believe that this book will change your life*!

Naturally I am fully aware of the pitfalls of making such an outrageous claim, and I do not wish to appear that I'm overstating the value of the book. However, the many hundreds of conversations I have had with dental professionals have led me to the same undeniable conclusion: *the area in which they require most help is discussing fees and dealing with price objections*. These are two absolutely fundamental issues which have ultimately led to regular undercharging of their patients. Almost without exception, dentists I've met have admitted that sometime during their practice lives, they have found this whole matter extremely uncomfortable.

This book reveals information on exactly how to deal with this problem. The contents are not taught at any dentistry school, and while certain elements of pricing may have been touched on by dental coaches, they'll have barely scratched the surface. I'll be looking at this complex issue in depth, delving into the psychology of what you do in those awkward situations and even why you do it!

I will attempt to improve not only your ability to tackle all pricing issues but also the ability of your team to support your efforts. I will alter your thought process, your beliefs, and most significantly, your behavioural pattern. You will never improve your results until you change your entire approach.

This book will enable you to smash through all the restrictions that you've placed upon yourself when it comes to the fees that you charge your patients. I guarantee that once you've broken your own barriers down, the methods described in this book will provide you with the confidence necessary to deal with every pricing issue which arises.

In truth it is quite understandable that you should feel uncomfortable when it comes to dealing with money. At dentist school you were taught how to deliver your specialist technical skills in a caring and empathetic manner. You have quite rightly been trained to be a health-care professional and not a business person.

Perhaps you've also been affected by the bad press which the dental profession seems to receive? The media will sometimes highlight dentists who've opted to leave the National Health Service (NHS) in the UK to concentrate on private practice. This decision is cruelly portrayed by thoughtless journalists as being greedy, leaving your profession unjustifiably tarnished. From the evidence I have gathered, I have actually concluded that the total opposite is true. In reality it is undercharging which is much more prevalent in dentistry!

Dentists on my courses have painted a very different picture to that of the media. They often describe practices which are struggling to keep pace with rising overheads and staff that require increased salaries to meet their own spiralling domestic bills. In some extreme cases I've even heard of dentists piling debt onto their credit cards in order to meet financial demands.

Yet despite this increasingly bleak picture, the same dentists are still finding it almost impossible to quote their prices accurately. They find themselves regularly reducing charges, on the assumption that otherwise their patients won't be able to afford them. They believe that by offering discounts, they will hear the word *yes* more often. Reductions of this nature are, in my opinion, totally unnecessary and actually border on stupidity!

It is this kind of misguided thinking that I want to change forever. Through this book I want to completely alter your ways, and in so doing have a major impact upon your working life. In order for this to happen I will need a small commitment from you:

1. Please have an open mind and be ready to embrace new ideas.
2. Do not allow any preconceived notions to prevent you from learning these new concepts. If you don't

like these new ideas, it does not mean that your patients won't either.

3. Please read each chapter more than once and underline or highlight some of the areas which you feel relate most closely to you.

4. At least do something! Successful people are doers who take action. I've yet to meet a successful person who simply hopes and prays as a business strategy.

5. Let your team read the book as well. Maybe read it together and discuss the strategies it sets out.

6. Invest in the video which accompanies this book. This is an excellent resource that will help you and your team make even greater progress.

Please also visit my website, www.ashleylatter.com, and sign up to my newsletter, which I produce fortnightly. It has ideas and techniques designed to make even greater improvements to your business.

In this book I will share some personal tales which have gone a long way towards shaping my own business. Those closest to me would probably describe me as a person who keeps private matters to himself. I often identify with the caveman from the book *Men Are from Mars, Women Are from Venus*, who slopes off to his cave to be alone at times of crisis. That is certainly not the case here. I want to be open and honest throughout. I believe that by doing this, I can offer insight into my inner beliefs and reveal the thought processes which have led me to the ideas I will impart.

I will also discuss tips from other industries, which I believe can be of great benefit to the dental profession.

I have always found that your own industry can adopt practices from others. It can be extremely beneficial to remain open-minded to outside principles. I will refer to other books which I highly recommend, and indeed to my own courses, in which, naturally, I hope you'll want to invest in the future. My aim is to provide the full range of products and services that I believe will have a significant impact on your business and even your personal life.

Here is an outline of the contents of the book:

In Chapter 1 I reveal that price is very rarely *the* issue when people make everyday purchases. There are a variety of examples which will clarify that the people who have the greatest difficulty dealing with prices are not those who are buying, but actually those who are selling the services.

Chapter 2 is my personal view on how people buy in a struggling economy. Most people are prevented from making an investment not because of the price but because they're not confident enough to make the decision. I will discuss how the media have created this climate of caution, when in reality the economic situation is a great deal more optimistic, and why this negative portrayal can influence our thinking. I also challenge you to decide which practice you want to be in: one which is successful or one which is failing.

Chapter 3 addresses the issue of dentists carrying out simple procedures without charging. Though laudable, I discuss the potentially serious financial consequences of this selfless act. You'll be alarmed how much lost revenue this equates to!

Chapter 4 describes how the majority of patients' decisions to invest are based upon their emotions and *not* their wallets. Dentists are largely technically minded. They will spend too much time on unnecessary scientific explanation and too little on the emotional side of the issue. I will demonstrate several examples which prove why people will always find the money for things that they really want.

In Chapter 5 I will reveal the greatest communication error dentists make in their everyday lives. I will explain the damaging consequences to your practice and the opportunities you will miss as a result. This chapter alone could save you thousands!

Chapter 6 looks at what your patients will be judging and equally what they won't. You'll be surprised by what you discover—it isn't what you may think. Patients don't mind paying higher prices, provided you have invested wisely in customer services, decor, and the environment. Perception is everything.

Chapter 7 is called 'You are worth it' and takes its name from the famous L'Oréal advert. I make you think about your achievements and how much you've invested and sacrificed to get to where you are today. I will share a number of personal tales which will hopefully inspire you.

Chapter 8 is all about the so-called 'screamer' patient. I will clarify what this category is and the significance of such behaviour. It explains how much damage can be inflicted by one person's negative feedback—if you allow it! There's a particularly personal example from my own career which will serve as a cautionary tale.

Chapter 9 looks at the importance of self-confidence. We're all aware of the significance of this most valuable of assets. I will offer a number of different ways in which we can boost our levels of this priceless commodity.

In Chapter 10 I demonstrate the importance of evidence, particularly in written and even in video form. I will describe how this is a vital marketing tool in an era when patients are shopping around more extensively than ever before.

Chapter 11 is all about figures and specifically how impactful a swing of as little as 10 per cent can have on your bottom line. On my courses, I usually find that when I discuss this issue, there are many dentists who look very sheepish!

In Chapter 12 the focus is on the language we use when presenting a treatment plan to the patient. Simplicity and clarity can make all the difference. I also look at how to create value in the eyes of the patient.

Chapter 13 demonstrates how we can compete with the practice down the road when they offer lower prices than we do. Competition is fierce, and with more patients shopping around, dentists are now asking how they can challenge their local rivals. Here I will share with you what you need to do in order to stand out from the crowd.

This brief outline indicates how much the book has to offer. It is concise yet packed with detail, and can be absorbed in just a few hours. An avid reader myself, I digest at least one business book a month. My aim is to concentrate on valuable ideas and useful strategies. I trust that you'll enjoy the contents here, implement them into your working life, and ultimately reap the benefits of what you've learned.

Here's one final request from me. I have invested a great deal of time and no little effort putting this book together. I would certainly welcome any feedback you may have. Whether the feedback is positive or negative, I hope it will be constructive. I'm a firm believer in being receptive to criticism, and any comments you can provide will be greatly appreciated.

Chapter 1

Is price the issue or an issue?

So is price the issue or an issue when you buy products and services? Here is a simple exercise to determine how important the price tag is when you make your own purchases. Firstly, get a piece of paper and write down five acquisitions that you have recently made: maybe an item of clothing, a meal out, or even a present.

Secondly, consider this: when you made these purchases, was the price the most important factor? Think carefully about your thought process. Only put a tick next to the item if you made your purchase decision solely based on price.

How many ticks do you have?

When we do this exercise on my programmes, we very rarely get anybody who has bought anything based on price alone. We could have twenty-five delegates, equating to more than one hundred purchases, and I would say on average per class, we get only a handful for which cost has been the most significant issue. There are always other, more important factors such as brand, colour, and design.

There are always, therefore, other, equally important considerations in addition to the cost.

Let's say you're buying a television. You might do some research on the Internet and visit several stores in order to determine which brand you like and which model would look best in your living room. Technology may be an issue too, as you decide whether to acquire a plasma screen, HD picture quality, or even 3D capability. Only once you have collated all that information will you begin to look into its potential price bracket.

The example above is from my own personal experience, but I usually find that the same principles also apply to business-to-business purchases. Think about the furniture and everyday materials you currently use in your surgery. When you bought them, was cost the number one factor, or were there other, more important considerations?

Now look at the day-to-day invoices you settle. Are they always for the cheapest products? Are there other factors such as service or the relationship you have with your supplier? How important was quality? When these items are discussed on my courses, though price is certainly an issue, it is never *the* issue.

Apply this same process to a vendor you no longer use. Did you leave that vendor because of price, or were there other, more important factors such as poor service, unreliability, or perhaps an irreconcilable breakdown in the relationship with the company or its representative?

My courses are attended by a variety of professionals with an ever greater array of salaries. Most practices bring their entire team onto my programmes. Regardless of their budgets, it is rarely the price alone which has been the decisive factor in determining their everyday purchases. Whether they are cautious or spontaneous, in my experience, it is never the price tag alone which has ultimately influenced the purchases they make.

Why not try this exercise with your staff? You will quickly learn how many different factors they will consider before they buy.

Imagine a world where price *was* the most important factor. Everyone would be driving the most basic cars, eating only cheaply made food, and wearing bargain basement clothing. There would be no need for luxury cars or Michelin star restaurants, while designer label stores would all be boarded up.

So far I have demonstrated that, while naturally important, price is by no means the most decisive factor. However, there are some exceptions for whom price will always influence their final decision.

So who buys solely on price?

In my experience there are four types of people who base their decision making solely on price.

Professional buyers

They are trained to buy on price only. They typically work for large department stores, where their job is to buy the best quality possible at the lowest price and on the best terms for their business.

People on limited income

They will buy on price because they simply have no choice. In my first year as a business coach, as I began to grow my client base, I had first-hand experience of basing all my decisions on cost alone. I quickly discovered that you always got more for your money when shopping for food at the end of the day, as some stores reduced the prices of certain items that were getting close to their sell-by date.

Those who are foolish

This may seem a little harsh, but there are some people I've met who are penny rich but pound foolish and in my opinion do not value their time.

An orthodontist openly admitted on one of my courses that he went to thirteen different shops, spread over two weekends, before he finally purchased a rucksack for £75 for a walking holiday.

Here was a highly skilled professional, with the potential to earn hundreds, maybe thousands of pounds every day, squandering more than ten hours of his valuable time to make a small purchase.

And he's not alone. A dentist on my course once admitted that he had travelled over fifty miles on long country lanes to save just £30 on seed for his garden—a saving which was surely negated by the extra petrol used and the extra hours wasted in getting there!

*People who have not been given a good enough
reason to invest.*

This is a group who are undecided and who do not yet feel they've received sufficient information to make a commitment. They might be comparing one practice's price with another's or perhaps weighing up a private option against one available through the NHS. In each case the patient will need a fuller explanation before choosing your particular procedure.

Invariably this lack of information has arisen due to a lack of sales and communication skills. An inability to fully explain the many benefits you have to offer has left the patient unwilling to proceed. I will address this significant problem in greater detail later in the book.

To summarise:

1. Price is always more important in the mind of the seller than in the mind of the buyer. While price is an issue, it is very rarely *the* issue.

2. When conducting the five-purchases exercise with your team, you will have concluded that very few purchases are solely price driven.

3. The most important skills you must develop are communication and ethical sales skills. I may of course be talking from a biased standpoint, but I'm sure I've now convinced you why these are so imperative.

Chapter 2

How people buy when times are tough

In the previous chapter, I demonstrated that when people make everyday purchases, whether of services or products, the decision to spend is never solely down to cost. Another myth concerns people's buying habits during the recession.

I write in 2013, in the fifth year of the current financial crisis. It's now the longest recession the UK economy has ever suffered. Currently we have one of the largest debts to GDP ratio in the Western world, and although the government has put so-called 'austerity measures' in place, the debt is still growing, with no apparent end in sight. It seems nobody knows how to get out of this mess!

Every day our media are bombarding us with negative messages, stating how bad the current situation is and how much worse it's going to be. And in the era of 24 hours a day, 365 days a year news channels, these messages are constant.

The growth of social media has served to exacerbate the problem still further. It's now almost impossible to avoid gloomy reports on the state of the economies of Europe. I honestly believe that there is an entire industry whose sole purpose is to increase our anxieties and ultimately our feelings of insecurity.

For example, have you ever known the opening story on a news programme to be about a company winning a major order and creating two hundred new jobs? Yet these things *are* happening—they're just not making the front pages of our newspapers or the lead items on our 24-hour news channels. In truth, good news does not sell.

This problem is by no means confined to the UK's media, as I witnessed for myself on a recent trip to Ireland, a country with its own economic plight.

Usually over breakfast I read the local newspapers, in order to gain a greater insight into the area in which I'm working and the unique problems it may face. This can be of great importance in preparation for a course delivery.

In this particular newspaper, the opening thirteen pages seemed dedicated to the recession and the impact it was having on the community. This was in addition to a tale about drug crime and even a murder! I was feeling pretty low by the time I reached the middle section of the paper.

However, on turning to the next page, my mood was somewhat transformed. I read a tiny article about a local engineering company which was taking on extra workers, having won a large overseas contract. At last some good news, albeit tucked away in a few lines and inconspicuous among the other tales of doom and gloom.

If only this had been featured on the front page, it would have had a significant impact on the spirits of the readership, at a time when the economic picture seems so bleak. I believe that burying positive stories in this manner is simply unacceptable!

Because of the way the newspapers portray their news, I rarely read newspapers nowadays, concentrating my reading on either personal development or business books. I often compare some newspapers to junk food. We all know that eating too much junk food is not good for your body and health. Yet when you read some newspapers, you are filling your mind with the same junk.

In reality are things as bad as they are being portrayed? Despite the downturn, there are still many businesses which are thriving, and others that are expanding. Many are increasing turnover, delivering profits, and creating new jobs in the process.

Take for example the German luxury car manufacturer Porsche. A friend of mine had to wait six months before he could take delivery of his new car. When he asked for a discount in lieu of the excessive wait time, all he received was a sarcastic grin and a firm shake of the head. I encountered a similar experience myself when buying a new Land Rover Evoque; another six months' waiting list, take it or leave it!

I recently read about a farm in Berkshire in the south of England (www.copasturkeys.co.uk), which sold more than 40,000 turkeys at Christmas, some with an astonishing price tag of £150! This is some fifteen times more expensive than at the supermarket, yet the farm continues to thrive. It could even boast that its online sales were up 4 per cent, while farm gate sales had risen by 8 per cent in 2013.

In a later chapter, I will make reference to this story again, as there are some very important lessons to learn regarding how this farm successfully distinguished itself from the competition in order to command such high prices. Some of these marketing strategies can certainly be transferred to dentistry. Trust me, there are some superb lessons we can take away from the farm which sells turkeys.

In fact the food industry can often act as the barometer in determining the real state of the economy. I always challenge the delegates on my courses to telephone the most expensive restaurant in town and attempt to book a weekend table. They always find such establishments to be either fully booked or offering unsociable times, such as six o'clock or eleven o'clock at night.

It's a similar situation in other industries too. Exclusive bespoke tailors Savile Row, have just reported that sales of their handmade suits have increased from the previous year. In 2012 alone they made in excess of twelve thousand individually tailored suits, at an average cost of some £2,800!

These kinds of encouraging figures are now also being seen in dentistry. Several of my clients in the north-west of England are reporting a bumper year; one dentist informed me that he now has to open on a Saturday morning to cope with demand from patients for implants. Many of these treatments run into many thousands of pounds.

I recently spoke with a practice manager who arrives at work at seven o'clock in the morning to deal with all the Internet enquiries she receives overnight. The practice has reported a record number of clients for orthodontic treatment. The figures they shared with me were frankly overwhelming! And this tale is by no means exclusive. Another practice informed me that they were taking on an extra associate because of the increased demand for private dentistry in the area. All these examples are in the north-west of England, supposedly one of the less affluent regions of the UK.

All these practices have three vital factors in common. All were proactive in how they marketed themselves, all were working extremely hard, and, significantly, all could boast staff with excellent communication skills.

When you look back at the old black-and-white newsreels of the 1940s, they depict an era where people were forced to queue for food. Thankfully the dark days of rationing are now behind us. It seems the longest queues these days are reserved for customers clamouring for the latest Apple iPhone or iPad!

Recently I was walking through London at eleven o'clock at night on Oxford Circus, where a large crowd was gathered outside a clothes shop. There must have been around two hundred people jostling with at least a dozen security guards attempting to keep them in order. On closer inspection it was the launch of a brand-new range of clothes by the pop star Rihanna. Despite the freezing weather—it was minus 3°—these people wanted to be the first customers in the country to own them!

There are many more instances like this which seem to suggest that the economic situation is improving. In March 2013 a reported 1.8 million people left the UK to go on holiday during the Easter break. Manchester Airport alone carried 12,000 more holiday makers than the equivalent weekend a year earlier. Though the British weather may have contributed to the exodus, it still points to a significant increase in people's willingness to spend their hard-earned cash.

It seems that things are nowhere near as bleak as the media would like you to think. Don't let their negativity influence your thinking and the decisions you make in your practice.

I often hear of dentists who haven't raised their prices for more than five years because they believe their patients may desert them if they do. This is a very worrying development. Their practices' costs have risen significantly, and without an increase in price accordingly, this can only lead to a reduction in profits. If the profits are reduced, then there will be no investment, and before you know it, these practices will deteriorate.

To end this chapter, I want to share a personal story with you that had a dramatic impact on my life and continues to do so more than twenty years later. It occurred in early 1993. I was in my second year as a Dale Carnegie careerist. My role was to market, promote, and sell Dale Carnegie courses in the Trafford Park area of Manchester. I was paid on a commission-only basis. If no one signed up to the courses, I made nothing. Is there a greater motivating factor?

In the early nineties the UK was also in the clutches of another deep recession, and I was really struggling to sell. My figures were poor and I could barely pay my bills. I was consequently summoned by my sales manager, David, who asked me two pertinent questions:

—Why are your figures so poor?
—What are you doing to improve them?

I blamed my poor results on the recession, the price of the courses, and the fact that no companies in my area were investing in their staff. Yes, I blamed the territory that I operated in. This list of excuses merely served to inflame David still further, and he proceeded to give me the greatest dressing-down of my life.

I was told that my other colleagues, whose territories included Liverpool, Lancashire, and Cheshire, were all flourishing; some were even boasting record figures. It appeared I was the only salesman who was failing!

It was then, however, that he told me something that had a profound impact on my career and is still of genuine significance twenty years later. He told me to 'stop taking part in the recession'.

While I was caught up in the recession's web, my colleagues were not. This realisation changed my thinking immediately. Almost overnight I became more positive, and in turn my results improved dramatically. I have never let bad news get the better of me since. I quickly learned to take full responsibility for my own results.

So if you have allowed the recession and all the bad news surrounding it to affect your thinking, you now have my permission to *stop taking part in it*!

To summarise:

1. The economy is struggling and is likely to do so for some considerable time. Accept the reality of the situation and adapt yourself accordingly.
2. Your clients' buying habits have changed irreversibly. Have yours?
3. Despite the economic climate, there are many companies and practices which are still thriving. It's now time to decide which direction you want to take. Only you can take responsibility for your results.
4. Don't be influenced by the newspapers' depressing portrayal of the recession. Better still, don't read them!
5. Avoid negative people. They can drag you down with them and are always generous in spreading their gloomy outlook.

Chapter 3

There will be no charge today

Imagine for a moment that you're at the checkout at your local supermarket. All your shopping is on the belt, and there's a very helpful staff member offering to assist you with both the scanning and packing of your groceries. As the items move towards the till, the checkout girl decides that she's not going to charge you for every fifth item she scans. She places the free items in a separate bag to highlight how much she's decided to give away. (I did say 'imagine'!)

Now here's another scenario. You are shopping in a top department store, buying clothes. You've bought a jacket, trousers, shoes, shirt, and tie. At the till, the shop assistant takes your trousers out of the bag and puts them into a separate one. She then turns to you and, with a broad smile on her face, happily states, 'I've decided that you can have the trousers for nothing!'

These two examples are little short of fanciful, yet on my courses, dentists regularly tell me of a number of simple procedures that they've conducted, for which they've decided not to charge their patients a single penny.

Have you ever carried out a basic cementing of a crown, a quick clean, or a tiny filling, and then taken the decision that the patient didn't need to pay for what you've just done? Do you do this regularly? If so, then this chapter will be of great significance, as I seek to change that mindset for good. You may find that this one section alone will save you a fortune in lost revenue.

The first question I always ask when I'm told about this charitable work is, 'Why do you do it?' One of the explanations offered by dentists that were once NHS but are now private is that it's a hangover from the days when simple procedures, such as fillings, were indeed free of charge for their patients. Having been accustomed to this way of working for many years, for these dentists it's a hard habit to break. If your entire private practice is staffed by former NHS dentists, there could well be a great deal of free work being carried out.

Another explanation offered is that, as it only takes a few minutes to complete such jobs, they don't seem to justify a charge. Dentists often add that they didn't think that their patients had the money anyway. This type of thinking is little more than an unfounded assumption, something I'll be looking at in greater detail in a later chapter.

One other popular explanation I hear concerns patients who've been with a practice for many years. Dentists feel that charging long-time patients for simple, quick procedures will create a negative response. There is even a belief that charging in these circumstances may prompt a previously loyal patient to look elsewhere for treatment in future!

In my experience it's actually the opposite which is true. People expect to be charged and feel uncomfortable when they're not.

Before exploring this further, I feel it important to point out that I realise there are occasions when offering something for nothing is entirely acceptable. I myself will conduct presentations without charge from time to time, and I will always happily give advice to clients when they've contacted me regarding a specific issue. However, this is not something I do habitually and is most often a result of significant previous investments or productive referrals. What I want to address here is the actual cost to a practice of regular, sometimes daily procedures which are conducted without charge.

I will begin by describing an example I was made aware of by a practice manager on one of my courses. She admitted that she had a problem with one of the dentists, who consistently carried out work without charging. She estimated that this amounted to around ten minutes of free work an hour.

Now let's put some figures to this situation. I will assume the dentist's earnings to be around £300 per hour. Ten minutes of that time would be worth £50. Let's assume further that he works for 35 hours per week and for 45 weeks per year.

In other words, this dentist is losing out on £50 per hour x 35 hours per week x 45 weeks per year. It equates to a staggering £78,750 of lost revenue per year for the practice! If that dentist worked for thirty years, he would effectively be carrying out more than two million pounds' worth of free dentistry! At this particular practice it was just one dentist, but can you imagine if there were two or three offering equally generous freebies?

As far as I'm aware, no practice has charity status. A practice is a fully fledged business with staff to pay and ever increasing costs to meet. An extra £79,000 would certainly be most welcome. An investment of that size in new equipment, for example, would be hugely beneficial. Pay rises for staff could be afforded more easily, and—dare I say it—Ashley Latter training courses could be paid for to increase the productivity of the entire practice!

The practice manager also revealed that when patients came to the reception desk afterwards, they were always surprised and puzzled that there was no charge, having already begun to bring out their purses or wallets.

In my experience, when people are given something for nothing, they very rarely appreciate it. For example, I read personal development, business, sales, and marketing books. It's somewhat of a hobby of mine and allows me to learn about new ideas and concepts which I can utilise. I lent a friend of mine one such book when he was suffering a personal crisis in his life. It was Dale Carnegie's *How to Stop Worrying and Start Living*, which I always recommend to anyone who is feeling stressed or anxious. I truly believed that it would help him get through his problems. But when I saw him next, he admitted that though his situation had worsened, he'd not had an opportunity to even pick up the book. It was a real shame.

This has occurred several times, and as a consequence I now rarely lend out my books. Unless a person has gone out and bought the book him or herself, there is rarely a commitment to try to do anything about the situation. I've concluded that, on the whole, people don't appreciate things that are free.

Another consequence of giving something away without charge is that people will start to expect it. It's very difficult to convince people to pay for something when they haven't had to in the past. Those dentists who have gone private after being in the NHS will be well aware of this.

One final point is that there are much greater assurances which come with charging for your services. When you know that money is coming in it's much easier to concentrate on what you're doing. You portray incredible self-confidence. If you are aware of bills which you're struggling to meet or salaries you may not be able to pay, the job becomes a great deal harder. I have been in a similar position before and I never want to be in that situation again.

During my research ahead of writing this book, I read Stuart Wilde's excellent book *The Trick to Money is Having Some* in which he purports the theory that the difference between having it and not is merely a small but subtle shift in consciousness. Within it he wrote
A chapter called 'When they show up, bill em' which certainly makes good sense to me.

To summarise:

1. Remember that you have thousands of pounds, hundreds of hours, and dozens of sacrifices invested in developing your skills. Make sure you charge for them!
2. Occasional freebies are fine only when your financial situation is secure. You'll feel much better about it then.
3. Remember, those seemingly insignificant ten minutes really do add up.

Chapter 4

People always find money for things that they want

In April 2008, I was incredibly fortunate to be at Old Trafford when my favourite football team, Manchester United, beat Barcelona in the European Cup Semi-Final. As the opponents were widely regarded as one of the best in history, it meant reaching the final that year was a remarkable achievement. As the momentous victory began to sink in, so too did the prospect of attending the final itself become ever more enticing. There was one significant problem, however: the final was being staged nearly two thousand miles away in the Russian capital, Moscow.

Usually tickets for such an illustrious occasion are almost impossible to find, but as this was a five-hour flight and a particularly expensive trip, demand wasn't as great as usual, even though the opposition was another English team, Chelsea. The cheapest package cost a staggering £1,300, with a basic itinerary which didn't include a hotel or even a match ticket!

Naturally most fans were put off, including many of my closest friends. But my desire to be there overcame my hatred of being ripped off, and I decided to go. (My wife still reminds me of the price I paid whenever she wants to invest in a new outfit.)

On reflection I have never regretted my decision. This was a special occasion involving a team I'd followed all my life, and my desire to be there far outweighed the financial expenditure and my more logical thought processes. This was the first ever all-English European Cup Final, it involved my team, and I really wanted to be there regardless of the cost.

The key word in all of this is 'want'.

On that night, there were 25,000 others who had made a similar emotional decision. As we mingled around Moscow, many exchanged stories of loans they'd taken out, overtime they had endured, or even family holidays they'd had to forgo in order to be there. It seemed that regardless of their disposable income, the importance of the occasion had won them over and forced their attendance, despite the impracticalities. It was clear that when somebody wants something badly enough, he will always find a way to pay for it. This is a most significant mantra.

There are many examples of this within dentistry. I recently chatted with a dentist at a modern practice in a working-class area of Glasgow, which mixed both NHS and private treatments. He'd previously attended my two-day 'Ethical Sales and Communication' programme along with his wife, who was his practice manager. They were extolling the virtues of the course and had already begun to see the benefits, with an increase in treatments, particularly orthodontic. I was delighted to hear that they'd already signed up as many as ten new cases in just six weeks.

They recalled in particular a young lady who worked at the local supermarket. She was embarrassed by her crooked teeth. A consultation revealed that she required treatment costing £2,500, which she said she simply couldn't afford. Determined to transform her appearance, however, she came back for a second consultation. With the assistance of the practice staff, she negotiated a bespoke monthly instalment plan which allowed her to pay £300 in cash at the start of each month.

In this case, the young lady felt that her teeth had so affected her self-confidence that she was determined to find a way of meeting the costs necessary to improve her appearance. Agreeing to a structured payment plan enabled her to realise that dream. The treatment had an enormous impact on her life and transformed her low self-esteem.

Another similar story I once heard from a dentist on my Two Day Ethical Sales & Communication Programme concerned a patient who was a refuse collector for a living. He decided to have two implants fitted six months before his wedding day, because he hated his dentures and wanted to look his best for the photographs.

Both these examples confirm that you should never make assumptions about a patient's disposable income, even if at first the costs may seem prohibitive. I go into more detail on this subject in the next chapter, possibly the most important in the book.

There will be many patients like these in your database, all of whom could be equally determined to improve their smiles. It's up to you to make the time to engage them in conversation and take an interest in their lives. It may just create a new business opportunity.

In my previous book, *Don't Wait for the Tooth Fairy: How to Communicate Effectively and Create the Perfect Patient Journey in your Dental Practice*, I described how patients buy cosmetic treatments emotionally. While naturally they employ logic too, it's never without emotional backup. The only way to determine what their specific emotional reasons might be is to engage in conversation with them.

Sadly, it seems that the simple yet powerful act of asking questions has become somewhat neglected in sales. I strongly believe that everyone has a hobby, interest, or pastime for which price is of secondary importance when they commit to a purchase. For me it is normally a football trip or a concert abroad; for my wife it is most definitely shopping for shoes.

Me and Elliott in Moscow, 2008

To summarise:

1, Be assured patients will always find money for things that they want. I find in life everyone has a want, for which money is always found.

2 Discuss this with your team at a staff meeting. Ask them what they truly desire in their lives and what they would always find money for. Price will very rarely be an issue.

3, It may well be that what your patients want is something that you provide in your surgery.

Chapter 5

The biggest communication
mistake dentists make

Imagine that you are walking into a high-class restaurant. Its decor is stunning. It has marble floors and its walls are adorned with the finest artwork. As you breathe in the magnificent aromas of the award-winning menu, you are approached by an impeccably dressed maître d'. You request a table for two by the window, but as you do so, you're aware that she is constantly looking you up and down, studying your appearance from head to toe. Rather than hand you a menu, she instead suggests that you may prefer to eat down the road at a nearby fast food outlet or at a cheaper restaurant. She informs you that there is no table available, despite there being only a handful of people being served.

Try to imagine how you would be feeling. Shocked and embarrassed, yet equally disgusted. While you may launch into a tirade there and then, what is absolutely certain is that it wouldn't be long before you were recounting this tale to family and friends. These days the story would then quickly spread beyond your closest circles via Twitter and Facebook, allowing dozens, perhaps even hundreds more to learn of how appallingly you were treated. The power of social media can never be underestimated. It can certainly help grow your profile and help to destroy it at the same time.

Though this may seem an extreme scenario, how many times a week are you guilty of similar prejudgment? How often have you made assumptions about a patient's finances, on the basis of how he was dressed or where she lived?

Having coached thousands of dentists throughout the world, I have heard many admit that they've been guilty of this too. In my opinion it's one of the biggest mistakes dentists make. They, like the maitre d', have drawn conclusions solely on the basis of appearance.

So what happens when you prejudge patients?

1. You may be costing yourself many thousands of pounds' worth of new opportunities for you and your practice.
2. By not making your patients aware of all the options, you will be denying them the opportunity to choose their favourite. You won't even be making them aware of your diverse range of treatments. Remember: as a matter of informed consent, it is important that you do mention all the options.
3. You will be missing out on delivering technical skills that you have probably spent hundreds of hours learning—skills which you may well have developed during weekends and nights away from

your family. Some of these courses will have cost you thousands of pounds, not to mention the amount of kit you will have invested in that will now have to remain pristine in its box!

4. You will never fulfil your true potential.
5. You might not fulfil the dreams of your patients.

Points 4 and 5 are, in my opinion, criminal.

One of the services I offer is an in-house course which is held at the client's practice. Normally on the day before, I will visit to observe their procedures and make recommendations. This will often involve me watching the dentist in consultation with his or her patients, once the patients' permission has been sought for me to do so.

During one consultation, it was clear that a genuine rapport had been built up between the dentist and his patient—a woman in her thirties dressed fairly casually in jeans and a jumper. She informed him that she was interested in having her teeth straightened as she was unhappy with her smile. She revealed that she'd had a similar treatment when she was a child, but because she rarely wore her retainers, the teeth had gone crooked once again. It would then cost her more money to repeat.

On hearing the word 'cost', the dentist launched into a lengthy explanation of all the payment options that were available, such as interest-free or low cost, longer term loans. Intriguingly the dentist had become so fixated with price that he never inquired as to what the woman wanted to alter or why she'd decided to embark on the same procedure now. Despite his examination of the woman's mouth, no treatment options were discussed, nor was there any further conversation about what changes the woman wanted to make.

On the way out, the dentist even advised her to pick up a leaflet regarding finance options. The patient, who came in with a problem, left the surgery with no potential solutions offered to her.

In this instance, I honestly believe that because of the casual way in which she was dressed and her reference to cost, the dentist had assumed that price would be the overriding issue in determining whether the woman would have her teeth straightened. In reality a potentially lucrative treatment plan had been allowed to slip away.

Even more galling was the fact that the patient herself had actually brought the problem to the dentist's attention. Think about it: the patient came in with a problem and she left with a problem. This was probably a perfect example of my belief that the person who had the biggest problem with the price was the dentist.

I have many more examples like this. Here is another which highlights one of the greatest sales crimes—*assumption*.

I recently delivered my 'High Impact Presentation Skills Programme', in which I coach twelve delegates how to deliver world-class presentations. It is an intense but thoroughly enjoyable programme utilising a video camera, and carries with it enormous satisfaction. A participant's progress can be literally life changing! *For more information on this course, please visit my website http://www.ashleylatter. com/high-impact-presentation-skills.html.*)

On this particular programme, we had a dentist who gave a presentation about a patient who was having a significant implant treatment, costing just under £10,000. The patient was in his late forties and was often dressed very scruffily. He always had a tired and gaunt appearance, and he would always pay for his treatment in cash with five-pound notes!

Naturally the practice staff became curious about this odd method of settlement and speculated as to the reasons why. Some even came to the conclusion that the patient must be a drug dealer, particularly as he usually arrived late and carried the money inside a plastic bag. When the patient finally completed the treatment, the staff were all quite relieved.

One Saturday morning a few months later, the dentist was at home when he received a knock on his door. To his enormous surprise, there stood the very same patient, standing there looking gaunt and tired. With all the discussion about his possible shady career, the dentist was particularly concerned about this unexpected visit. He nervously asked the man why he'd come to his home and whether he'd had any problems with his teeth?

The patient responded with a beaming smile and stated how delighted he was with his teeth. This only served to increase the dentist's anxiety, however. He was still unclear why the man had visited him first thing on a Saturday morning.

His fears were allayed when the patient declared, 'I clean all the windows in your street, and I was wondering whether you wanted me to do yours? I only charge a fiver for the whole house!'

So much for the drug dealing theories! Another inaccurate assumption had been well and truly dispelled.

Every once in a while you hear a phrase which sticks in your mind forever. One such phrase for me is 'prescription before diagnosis is malpractice'. It's had such an impact on me that not only do I adhere to it myself, but I also deliver its message to all my clients. It reiterates the invaluable directive that you must never offer a solution without first finding out what the patient actually wants.

Assuming is one of the most unforgivable mistakes which dentists make and yet the most commonly made one too. Imagine going to a doctor and informing him or her of your medical problem. Without any further questioning or examination, you are handed a prescription that will supposedly solve your problem. How would you feel? Would you trust the doctor's recommendations and advice?

In recent times I have seen a sharp increase in the number of NHS dentists who are now coming to me for coaching, seeking to improve their sales of private treatments in their practices. I believe this is becoming ever more essential, as NHS funding is not being increased while the costs associated with running a practice most definitely are. Dentists are consequently looking at new revenue streams in order to keep themselves afloat.

For those who are now moving towards private alternatives, here's some valuable advice: it is imperative not to make any assumptions regarding whether a patient will choose the private option. Any prejudgment on your part will effectively deny your patients one or more genuine options without them ever knowing it. As a consequence you will be missing out on many lucrative opportunities, while the people who'll be suffering the most will be the patients themselves, as they won't even be aware of all the possibilities. This is a heinous sales crime!

In my opinion, it is not up to the dentist to decide what the patient can or cannot afford; patients must decide for themselves. Present all the options with the same enthusiasm and passion, and allow the patient to make the choice. You must communicate enthusiastically and with the patient's best interests in mind. Only then can the patient make an informed decision.

Express the benefits of each option fully. Perhaps even present some evidence in the form of photographs or diagrams. Focus your communication on what advantages there will be for the patient. Make sure not to talk too technically, so as not to blind the patient with science.

If done well, I believe you will see a significant increase in the number of patients taking up your private treatments. This is absolutely vital; I have devoted a whole chapter to this topic in this book.

That said, it is imperative that you must *never* dismiss or criticise the NHS, as that would be very unprofessional. You should never bite the hand that feeds you.

It is also important to realise that along the way, some patients will still say no. Accept it and move on. That the last patient didn't take up an option will have absolutely no bearing on the decision of the next patient.

On encountering a negative response, many dentists seem to take it personally. It consequently affects the way in which they communicate to the patients that follow. Never take a no personally. It is unlikely to reflect anything you've done wrong. There are a number of reasons why a patient does not take up a treatment plan; you must continue to consult and present with the same passion and enthusiasm.

Remember: you are in show business. You are in business, and you are on show. The next patient who walks into your surgery may never have seen the act before.

In concluding this chapter, I want to tackle another area in which the assumption rule also needs to be addressed— the reception desk. I have visited many practices where a patient has queried a price at reception, and the receptionist has adopted the presumed point of view of the patient and not that of the practice.

I have heard receptionists utter phrases such as, 'It is expensive', or 'I know it's a lot of money', or 'I would go away and think about it if I were you'. Most damaging of all, I've even heard the response, 'Yes, you can have a holiday for this amount'.

In the majority of cases in which patients query a price, they are actually seeking reassurance that they are making the right decision. Any negativity from the receptionist can dissuade them from proceeding. I often seek such assurances from shop assistants when buying clothes. I can be indecisive in these circumstances, and a positive reaction from an attentive salesperson can ultimately convince me to buy.

One conclusion I've drawn regarding why a receptionist may adopt a negative stance is that the receptionist is basing his or her opinion on the cost, as if the receptionist were making the purchase. Though it is the patient who is considering an implant treatment costing £2500, the receptionist may think of it as a purchase that they are actually making. In that mindset, the receptionist makes the assumption that the cost could be difficult for the patient.

While I think we may all be guilty of this mistake from time to time, it is not our position to make an assumption about another person's finances. Let the patients decide for themselves.

To summarise:

1. Never make assumptions. Do not be influenced by how a person is dressed, where he lives, or what she does for a living.
2. Remember the golden rule, 'Prescription before diagnosis is malpractice'. Never offer the solution without first finding out the patient's requirements. If you do this often, you are making the biggest communication mistake in dentistry.

3. Treat people how you would want to be treated. Let the patients decide how they spend their money. It is their choice, not ours.

Chapter 6

What patients can judge . . . it's not what you think it is

Pretend for a moment that you are walking through an upmarket department store such as John Lewis or House of Fraser if you are reading this book outside the UK, think of an up market Department Store in your town. You see a wooden lacquered tea tray for sale. Depicted on its surface is a classic scene from the Lake District on a summer's day. There is a beautiful lake, a few ducks swimming, and a man fishing from a boat. In the background there are some large, impressive mountains.

What would you estimate would be its price? When I run this exercise on one of my courses, the delegates normally say between £60 and £80.

Now imagine you saw the same item on sale at a car boot sale, amid a host of other items on a table. (For people reading this book outside the UK, a car boot sale is a form of jumble or rummage sale. People gather in a parking area and sell used items from the backs of their cars.) What would you guess would be its price now? This time the delegates usually guess it to be nearer £3.

Finally, picture the same tea tray on sale at the world-famous London store Harrods, and again conduct the same exercise. This time estimates may be as high as £200. It is the exact same tea tray that was on sale at John Lewis and the car boot sale, yet in Harrods the estimated price was some sixty-six times greater than at the cheapest venue.

So why do we assume such an enormous discrepancy on price?

The obvious answer is the expectation that comes with an exclusive, high class Knightsbridge store. The manner in which the tray is presented, the customer service, the brand, and the famous green bag all conjure up a feeling of luxury, which an old table by the side of a car on a wet Sunday morning most definitely can't!

The significance of this exercise is to highlight that when it comes to selling products or services, everything matters. If you are charging premium prices, then every aspect has to be right. The customer service, the way in which the telephone is answered, and the surroundings in your practice will all have a bearing.

Here is an example to emphasise the point. A few years ago I ran a two-day 'Ethical Sales and Communication' programme in a three-star hotel in the centre of Manchester. The hotel boasts one of the best health clubs in the North-West and is situated in a popular tourist area, close to the canal.

The programme had gone very well. On completion many delegates stayed to socialise, exchange numbers, and embark on some useful networking. Once everyone had left, I reviewed the feedback sheets. Of twenty-seven delegates, twenty-six of them rated the programme either 9 or 10, except one who'd scored it at just 5. The low-scored feedback also had some derogatory comments about the two days. The contrast to the others was marked. I was a little taken aback.

On returning home that evening I continued to agonise over this stinging criticism. I even showed it to my wife, such was the effect it had on me. She rightly pointed out that it was very much the exception and told me to focus on the twenty-six who'd enjoyed the programme, not the one who hadn't. However, as I am a perfectionist, try as I might I couldn't ignore it. I endured an awful night's sleep.

The next morning, a Sunday, I went for a long, bracing walk in the park with my dog to get some fresh air and to focus my thoughts. I concluded that I had to telephone the client who had rated the course so poorly, in order to better understand his criticism.

It wasn't an easy call to make, and I was nervous as I dialled. However, my fears were quickly calmed as we chatted pleasantly for some time about the programme. He told me that he had actually loved it and went as far as to admit that it had been one of the best that he and his associate had ever taken. I was now even more puzzled about the low marks.

In the end I managed to discover the source of his discontent. It was the hotel! He said he hadn't enjoyed his stay, the food was poor, and he'd been woken up twice in the night by noisy guests returning from a late night out. He even added that my programme deserved a much better venue.

I was certainly glad that I had made the call and learned an invaluable lesson in the process. However good the course and however well received its content, delegates would judge the experience on every aspect of the two days they were in attendance. Everything matters. The food, the surroundings, the customer service—it all has a part to play. All businesses need to be aware that they too will be judged in the same way.

For example, how many times have you been impressed by the food in a restaurant, only to have your decision to return there change dramatically when you see the state of its toilets? It makes you think that if this is the way they look after the bathroom, maybe the standard of the kitchen's hygiene is similarly lax.

In your profession many patients won't necessarily be able to judge the standard of your dentistry as easily as they can the customer service and the overall experience. They will notice the surroundings, the waiting room, and the manner of your staff, and make their judgments accordingly.

A few years ago I received an enquiry from a dental practice near to where I live. The owner was interested in taking part in my two-day 'Ethical Sales and Communication' programme. She explained that while she'd taken several cosmetic courses and had recently completed a year-long implant course, she still struggled to communicate with her patients.

Due to the close proximity of the surgery, I asked if I could visit her and learn a little more about her concerns and, equally, what she was hoping to gain by taking my programme. She was delighted that I would take the trouble to meet her.

On arrival I have to admit that I was shocked by what I saw. The reception area decor was shabby, and its walls were cluttered with a plethora of different signs, which seemed to be sloppily held up by pieces of Blu Tack. (This is one of my pet hates. I believe that a dental surgery should be more professional than to slap up its information messages and posters with bits of coloured plasticine!)

Further inspection revealed thousands of brown patient files behind the surgery, no computer system, and even steel bars on the windows. There was almost no attempt to brighten the place except for two pictures hanging on the walls, one of an elephant and the other of a tiger. Both seemed as though they had been bought cheaply from a charity shop.

It all led to us having a very frank and honest conversation in which I was forced to reveal some home truths. I explained that in order for her to sell high-class cosmetic dental work, her environment had to exude similar high standards. I urged her to invest in her decor as soon as possible. I believed that improvements to her surgery, allied to the lessons on my programme, would enhance her selling skills immeasurably.

I always encourage my clients to have a team meeting and discuss in detail the surroundings in which they deliver their dentistry. Look at the building, the signage, the reception area, the décor, and even the bathrooms. Better still, do this with an outsider who doesn't work in your practice. An impartial opinion is always beneficial. We usually spend too much time in our practices to even notice the wallpaper coming off the walls or the tired-looking pictures in our waiting rooms. Along with Blu Tack, pictures of lions, tigers, and sunsets should also be banned from the walls of dental practices.

In my view, patients don't really notice how good the dental chair is or how effective your materials are to work with, but they can and do judge the decor and the environment. If you want to charge higher prices for your services, then the surroundings need to reflect that sense of quality. If you want to charge Harrods' prices, then your practice needs to feel more like a swanky Knightsbridge store, with of course high-class West End customer service offered by your staff.

One of the few downsides to my busy schedule is the number of times I have to stay away from home. I once worked out that in an average year I spend 125 nights in hotels! Naturally I have a whole range of tales to impart about the establishments in which I've stayed, but there's one experience in particular that highlights the importance of having a first-class team. Just one individual can damage everybody's reputation.

It occurred during a two-day Ethical Sales & Communication Programme I was delivering in North Manchester. I was heartened by the reaction of the delegates taking part. It was clear that improvements were already evident. As we were concluding, I realised that we had run over our expected finish time by ten minutes. My enthusiasm had got the better of me.

Suddenly one of the hotel staff burst into the room without knocking at the door. Not content with the rude interruption, she then launched into an angry tirade, in which she stated that we should have finished ten minutes earlier and that another group were soon arriving. She added that she would need time to tidy up before their arrival and promptly stomped out of the room, slamming the door behind her.

My delegates responded by grabbing their belongings, donning their jackets, and filing quickly out of the room. As we hadn't quite finished yet, I attempted to stop them by shouting them back. None had yet filled out the feedback sheets. Try as I might, I couldn't compete with the anger displayed by the woman from the hotel. It was a truly chaotic and unseemly end to what had otherwise been a very successful two days.

Needless to say I have never returned to the hotel, but the whole debacle did have a positive impact on my career. Having contemplated for many months over whether to invest in a new training centre, this sorry affair finally convinced me that the time was right to have my very own venue. In 2012 I purchased a building in Manchester, where I deliver the majority of my programmes. Frankly

I've never looked back. It has been one of the best business decisions I have ever made.

This story is designed to stress the importance of every single member of your staff. You may have a dozen in your team, but if only one has a bad attitude or a discourteous manner, the whole business can suffer. This is a person I refer to as the 'sales prevention officer' or SPO for short. These people need to be weeded out of your practice, although with employment law heavily on the side of the employee that is not easy.

In the case of this hotel, the two days prior to the last few minutes had gone extremely well. The food and refreshments had been delivered on time and were of good quality; our treatment by other members of the staff was largely professional and polite. The lasting impression, however, will be of that unforgettable tirade!

One business which is clearly aware of the significance of each member of staff portraying a good image is the Walt Disney Company. I was lucky enough to spend a week in Disneyworld with my family a few years ago, enjoying all its theme parks. Everything about it impressed me. Firstly, it was spotlessly clean. There was a constant array of staff mopping up floors, picking up litter, and being generally attentive to the overall cleanliness of the whole area. There were even people assigned to sweeping up any leaves that had fallen off the trees. They appeared to actually enjoy doing this.

Secondly, those who were working on the rides seemed consistently enthusiastic, whether it was first thing in the morning or last thing in the evening. However they may have felt inside, their passion never wavered and their smiles never altered. While a great deal of the guests' days were spent queuing, the cast members, as employees were described, managed to keep us smiling and in many ways contributed to the overall enjoyment of the holiday.

Disney has the enviable knack of encouraging us to spend significant amounts of our money without it impacting our positive feelings. A classic example of this can be found in its many souvenir stores situated at the end of each ride. All are unavoidable and filled with attractive displays which no child can possibly ignore. The tills are constantly ringing as parents are forced to succumb to their children's demands. While Disneyworld is basically just another theme park, it manages to create an unforgettable experience through its variety of rides and colourful parades. (On a separate issue, if you are planning a trip to Disney and are worried about the cost of all the gifts that you think you will purchase for your children, then give your children their spending money up front and allow them to make their own purchasing decisions. It worked really well for me.)

I don't wish to create the impression that these excellent standards of customer service apply only in the States. I have encountered many examples of similarly attentive staff here in the UK, most notably at the Linthwaite Hotel in Windermere, which I visit with my wife regularly to walk and unwind. Here too, their standards are exceptional. Year after year the hotel has portrayed the same high standards, which demonstrates the importance of being consistent all the time. Once standards have been set, they must be maintained.

One practical way of demonstrating to your staff how significant excellent customer service can be is by offering to take them to an exclusive restaurant as a reward for reaching certain targets. Make sure it's somewhere renowned for its exceptionally high standards. On returning to the practice, discuss the experience with the team. Ask them to note down what they felt was particularly outstanding and see if some of these ideas can be adopted by the practice. In an exceptionally productive year, why not even take them all to Disneyworld!

To summarise:

1. Patients will not judge the dentistry as much as they will judge the customer service, decor, and environment. If you want to charge higher fees, then you must look into these vital factors first.

2. Seek an outside opinion regarding the way patients perceive your surgery. Perhaps even use a mystery shopper to write a report. We are too close to our businesses to see what needs changing.

3. Take your team on a fact-finding mission with a difference. Treat them to a top-class restaurant where they can observe high standards of customer service and think about what aspects they too can adopt.

Chapter 7

You are worth it

The hair and beauty company L'Oréal uses the slogan 'You're worth it' to publicise their products. The latest glamorous star to utter this line is singer Cheryl Cole. But how can we apply this catchy advertising slogan to dentistry?

Through the next section of the book I want to share with you some very personal stories that have shaped my life. They explain how I became involved in business coaching and, more specifically, dentistry. While I have touched on the subject matter before, I will now go into much greater detail in order to convey the contrasting highs and lows that I have experienced.

In 1991 I completed a fourteen-week Dale Carnegie course, which prompted me to join the company the following year. The job involved selling American training programmes in the Trafford Park and Salford areas of Greater Manchester. As I mentioned in an earlier chapter, this was on a commission-only basis, which meant that without a sale I earned nothing. In truth I have to admit that there were several fruitless weeks in which I struggled to make ends meet.

Before this career change, I had worked for a finance company for ten years. The position was the definition of secure, with an attractive salary of £25,000 a year. It afforded me a comfortable lifestyle and a BMW parked proudly on my driveway. The nineties had begun with a crippling recession, and my friends and family were astonished that I chose that moment to give up my settled existence.

If you aren't familiar with the Dale Carnegie organisation, they are a successful training company operating in around 80 countries worldwide across 275 franchises. They are renowned for having some of the best trainers in the world. At the time, they were definitely the market leaders in their field. Their brand was extremely strong.

While the founder's name may not be one you're familiar with, his bestselling book, *How to Win Friends and Influence People*, will surely ring a bell. Carnegie's iconic text is one which has impacted millions of people's lives. It is certainly something I would recommend you read as soon as the opportunity arises. In my opinion it is still the best book ever written on how to deal with people.

My role within the Carnegie franchise was a great deal humbler, however. I cold-called companies in my area, attempted to make appointments, and ultimately promoted the Carnegie courses. My first year was an utter disaster with a total income of just £8,000. Financially I was in a mess!

Most of the programmes I promoted took place in the evening. Twice a week I took the role of team coach, assisting the main instructor in course delivery. In addition, every Saturday I trained to become a course leader in my own right. It was incredibly challenging and was essentially designed to take participants out of their comfort zones, to demonstrate how they reacted. Ahead of each session I was filled with trepidation. I will never forget the instructor, Brendon Fitzmaurice, who pushed us to our limits. It felt like SAS training. Of the twelve who started the course, only five of us actually passed it.

After eighteen months of intense training, I was ready to deliver my own course, the first of which would be conducted over a weekend, under the careful scrutiny of a master trainer. If he was satisfied with my performance, I could proceed. Thankfully I passed first time and was given the go-ahead to advance on my own. After 600 hours of unpaid and rigorous training, I felt as much relief as I did elation.

Within three years I was delivering four sales courses a week in the North-West of England, many in Salford, a few miles from my home. I had a real passion for the programme, to the extent that I studied sales and marketing as a hobby, not simply for work. To this day it remains a keen interest, sometimes an obsession.

I clearly had an aptitude too, as my results matched my commitment. Of the 1,600 Dale Carnegie careerists throughout the world, I was often in the top five, not only for my sales but equally for the volume of courses we were delivering. Our results were regularly monitored, and it always amused me to see where our humble local City of Salford was placed in the worldwide league tables:

1. New York
2. Salford
3. Hong Kong
4. Chicago
5. Sydney
6. Munich

My work received worldwide recognition, and I was often chosen to speak at the international Dale Carnegie conference, both within small group workshops and on the main stage in front of the other delegates. My progression ultimately elevated me to become an international master trainer, the highest level that could be awarded to a Dale Carnegie careerist. This exclusive position required me to coach other trainers for six weeks each year, all over the world. It was a role which I thoroughly enjoyed.

I have listed these achievements, not to brag about what I've done, but to explain the journey I've taken. I have certainly hit rock bottom, but through determination and honest, hard graft, I have been able to realise many of my goals. I have committed to hundreds of hours of arduous training and spent thousands of pounds educating myself along the way. It all means that when I quote my prices, I feel justified in reciting the magical words, 'I am worth it'.

Here's an exercise that I would like you to do. It will take no more than ten minutes out of your day, but I can assure that it too will be worth it.

Write down the following:

1. The list of courses that you have attended.

2. The number of weekend courses that you have been on.

3. The list of qualifications that you have achieved.

4. The number of nights you have spent away from home studying, learning new techniques and gaining more knowledge, so that you can do your job more effectively.

5. The amount of money you have invested in your education.

6. The number of courses you are booked on in your current diary.

Are you surprised by the results? Are there a great deal more courses and hours and money than you thought?

Now try to factor in accommodation and travel expenses. In addition, work out how much surgery time you've lost in the process and therefore how much income that might have yielded. Finally and perhaps most significantly, calculate how many hours you've had to spend away from your family—time which, regrettably, you'll never be able to have back. It all adds up to a great deal of investment, both financially and emotionally.

This exercise will allow you to reach the conclusion that you've earned the right to charge the prices that you do. Many of the dentists who attend my courses admit to occasionally undercharging some of their patients. They have a reluctance to quote the tariff which their specialist work deserves. It is worth remembering that you possess a range of skills that very few people can boast.

On a course recently, one dentist admitted to the group that he often quoted a price that was 30% a treatment's value. He would do this on a range of different treatments over a year; this equated to thousands of pounds unnecessarily squandered. As he'd been in dentistry for twenty years, that effectively meant more than a million pounds in lost revenue—a sobering thought.

In my twenty years of coaching dentists, it still baffles me as to why so many admit to similar undercharging. One explanation is perhaps that dentistry school doesn't include any business lessons within its syllabus. However, even accepting that this is the case, dentists must surely realise how much time and effort that they have invested in themselves. Each dentist has made some serious sacrifices in life; it's now time to charge the level of fees which that commitment justifies.

I implore you not to make the same mistake that one clinical dental technician admitted to me: he had reduced the price of a set of dentures by 15 per cent simply because the patient used a bike to travel to the surgery.

The technician's mind was apparently made up when he saw that the patient had even kept his bicycle clips on his trousers during the consultation! The technician committed that most fundamental of errors and judged the patient by his appearance. What if that patient was an eccentric millionaire who simply liked riding bikes?

To summarise:

1. Stop and think of the numerous sacrifices you've made to reach where you are today. Remember the many years of study and the level of technical skill you can boast as a result. You possess a highly specialised talent.
2. Feel comfortable uttering my motto (and that of Cheryl Cole)—when it comes to setting the price, '*I am worth it.*'

Chapter 8

The screamer

As I'm sure you've already noted from the previous chapters, I have a number of personal anecdotes to share which I believe can offer valuable and relevant lessons. Here is another.

Several years ago I was asked to present at the British Dental Association–London Chapter on an extremely warm July evening. It was scheduled to last for two hours between seven and nine o'clock. Perhaps as a result of the stunning weather, the venue was packed, and the atmosphere at the reception beforehand was buoyant. I was very much looking forward to delivering my presentation.

The British Dental Association has a large conference room in the basement. As I began to talk, I realised that every seat had been taken, leaving many of the attendees to stand up at the back. It represented an excellent opportunity for me to describe the benefits of my 'Ethical Sales and Communication' programme to an attentive audience.

It seemed to be going well, until suddenly after about fifteen minutes, a gentleman sitting near the front and dressed smartly in a three-piece suit started to challenge what I was saying. While I don't recall his exact objections, I'll never forget the noisy and abrupt manner in which he presented them.

In twenty years as a business/sales coach, this had never happened to me before. I did my best to answer his concerns, but try as I might, he couldn't be satisfied by my answers. Perhaps understandably, it threw me completely off my presentation. I had no idea where I was up to or what I'd already said. I had never felt as awkward as this in my entire career, and I never wanted to feel that way ever again!

Somehow I managed to regain my composure and, by calling upon all my years of experience, resurrected my presentation. As I proceeded I was always mindful of my heckler, and I knew my words lacked their usual flow. Minutes later, my worst fears were again realised when he stood up to interrupt me for a second time. On this occasion, not content with challenging me, he even tried to encourage others within the room to agree with his objections!

The tension within the room was so great that initially there was an eerie silence. Then, to my horror, two further hands went up from a couple of elderly gentlemen dressed similarly to my heckler, in suits and bow ties. While the rest of the room retained their silence, I did what I could to answer the criticism. As I tried to clarify my views, I was equally aware that it was still not even eight o'clock. There was more than an hour to go before I could sit down.

How I got through the remainder of my slot, I do not know, but, aware of the significance of the opportunity, I felt I had no choice but to continue. As I reached the nine o'clock finishing line, I was thankfully greeted by a noisy round of applause. Bearing in mind what had occurred, this came as a very pleasant surprise.

Despite this positive end, the whole experience had been so disconcerting, that in my hotel room later that night, I was actually physically sick. The stressful events of my evening were proving difficult to overcome. Indeed, for the next two weeks, I was unable to rid myself of the image of the heckler in the bow tie. Whenever I subsequently gave a talk, I anticipated further heckling. I even began to offer apologies in advance to anyone who might not agree with my presentation.

By this point, I have to admit that I was even contemplating ending my career as a business coach. However, for reasons I couldn't quite explain at the time, I began to read through all my testimonial letters. I had accumulated hundreds over the years, and as I read through the lovely words people had written about me and my courses, it brought tears to my eyes.

Many described my courses as 'life changing', and I soon understood that many hundreds, if not thousands of clients were now achieving results they had previously thought were impossible. The more I read the letters, the more convinced I became that I shouldn't allow one rude heckler to destroy my self-belief, particularly as this had never happened before in my previous twenty years as a coach.

As I assessed my career, I calculated that I had delivered many thousands of hours of presentations all over the world. My diary was full of future bookings too. I knew it was time to halt my negative thought process and move on.

I pictured the heckler in the bow tie bawling down my ear and then imagined flicking him away off my shoulder. That symbolic act felt wonderful. I can honestly say that once he'd been swatted away, my life returned to normal. I had silenced my troublesome screamer once and for all.

Do you have a screamer who sits on your shoulders, giving you negative feedback all the time? If you have, my advice is never to focus on your screamer. He can occupy your every thought and take your mind off issues that are far more pressing and a great deal more significant. As I've got older, I know that I've also hardened my attitude towards negativity and those who would otherwise undermine my progress.

We will all encounter a screamer from time to time. The key is simply to accept that old adage that 'you can't please all of the people all of the time'.

For dentists the screamer might well be a patient who, on discovering the price of a treatment, replies with a sarcastic comment designed to make you feel you've overcharged. An example might be: 'I suppose I am paying for your new car am I?' or 'Now I know how you can afford to go on holiday three times a year!' I have heard this kind of comment recounted by many dentists throughout my coaching career.

It is vital to put this screamer into context. Though it is thoroughly unpleasant to hear such comments even once, think about the number of times you have heard them during your career. When you assess the number of consultations you have conducted, this extreme example surely represents just a tiny minority. Isn't it also possible that the patient's comments were made entirely in jest? In reality, we remember these comments because they are the exception and not the rule.

On one of my two-day 'Ethical Sales and Communication' programmes at my new training centre in Manchester, we had reached the section about money and price when one dentist told the group about his experience. His practice was based in a picturesque village in Lancashire, in the North of England, and his screamer was a patient who had been coming to see him for more than ten years. During that period, the patient had saved all his receipts and was fully aware of the prices he'd paid for his treatment. He had even collated the information into a file! Each time he attended an appointment, whether with the dentist or hygienist, he would make that caregiver aware of his vast collection of receipts.

This gentleman was the textbook definition of a screamer. Moreover, the dentist admitted that the screamer's complaints had had an impact on every price the dentist quoted to his other patients too. He regularly undercharged for almost all procedures. This pattern continued over a ten-year period, which must have equated to a staggering amount of lost revenue. In a later chapter, I will study the figures in greater detail using the so called "ten percent rule" but the estimated figure will be in the thousands and all because of one awkward patient.

My advice in this situation would be to insist that the patient find another practice. The dentist, though, was wary of doing so, as he was concerned with what the screamer might say within the local community. In my experience, screamers usually mix with like-minded people, and the likelihood is that you wouldn't want more screamers at your practice anyway. There would therefore be nothing to worry about in moving this patient on.

Another example came from a dental technician who told me that he never visited new clients, because his brother-in-law told him that his sales skills were poor. In my opinion, not visiting clients was seriously holding back the expansion of his business. His brother-in-law, as it happened, was an engineer working for a large multinational. Although I have nothing personal against engineers, you have to be careful whom you take your business advice from. Personally, I take advice from people much smarter than me, who have done it and got the T-shirt.

Having digested these examples of screamers, it's quite likely that you will recall situations in which you have dealt with similar characters. If this is the case and they are affecting your everyday dealings with other patients, then you must act quickly to rid yourself of a potentially damaging situation. Screamers have the ability to linger for several years if no decisive action is taken. It is important to flick them away.

Remember that in the vast majority of cases, money hasn't ever been the real issue, despite what the screamer may want you to believe.

To summarise:

- If you have a screamer in your life, work hard to rid yourself of him.
- Think carefully about what you say, as it can influence others. Communication is a powerful tool. For example if you tell your children to stop asking stupid questions, they will! This is the greatest skill you can bestow on your children.

Chapter 9

The importance of developing
self-confidence

In the previous chapter on screamers, I described how to deal with someone who makes derogatory comments about your prices. When this happens it can affect your self-confidence and seriously threaten your overall well-being. In this section I will focus on being positive and how to develop self-confidence that can benefit you in all aspects of your life.

Firstly I want to explore self-confidence in greater detail as, in my opinion, it is the key to success. Our perception of ourselves actually has an overwhelming impact on how others view us too. The more self-confidence we possess, the likelier we are to succeed. Without confidence it is almost impossible to thrive. It determines how many of our targets we will ultimately reach and affects our overall happiness, not just in business but in our everyday lives.

If we aren't feeling good about ourselves, our patients will notice. That will make it unlikely that we'll be able to charge the prices that our specialist services deserve. Those who are self-confident and positive exude those feelings and will in turn make their patients feel the same way. In that frame of mind, patients are much more likely to wish to proceed with treatment and at the prices that those services are worth.

Here are some of the characteristics of a person who is self-confident:

- Motivational
- Possesses a willingness to take risks
- Has an eagerness to stretch himself or herself
- Positive mindset
- Clear direction in life
- Clarity around values
- Acceptance of personal weak points and faults
- Indifference to what people think
- Strong self-belief
- Excellent interpersonal skills
- Belief in personal skills and talents
- Discipline
- Heightened self-awareness
- Ability to be consistent and persistent
- Credibility
- Self-responsibility
- Constant interest in improving
- Genuine interest in people
- Great listeners

I once heard a description that 'self-confident people operate south of arrogance'.

When I'm delivering my programmes or presenting at a conference, I am sure that most delegates think I'm a natural and that I was born with self-confidence. The reality is a great deal different. Like everyone else, I have to work at this on a daily basis. I can assure you that there are times when my levels dip and negative feelings edge into my psyche. When this happens I know it is up to me to fight back. Here are some of the methods I regularly employ in order to retain my self-confidence.

Have you ever wondered why some people are more successful than others? Why is it that some can get on with their lives while others seem to just stumble along? There are a number of factors which determine why this is the case, and one of the most significant is their level of self-confidence. I often refer to the *comfort zone*, an area of our lives where we will feel most at ease. It could be while carrying out the jobs we enjoy, speaking to the people we like, or staying in places that make us feel warm and relaxed.

Outside of our very own utopias, it's a very different story! We are faced with tasks which we hate and have to converse with people who make us feel uneasy. We feel challenged in situations which make us feel cold and on edge. It is even possible that one moment we are in our comfort zones, only to be suddenly and abruptly propelled out of them. This can be caused by something as simple as a client raising a price objection.

This kind of sudden rude awakening makes us wish we were back inside once again. But the problem with staying for too long in our comfort zones is that it becomes harder and harder to go out. The longer we reside there, the higher we build the walls around us. Before long, we're trapped!

I believe that the most successful people in life are the ones who are prepared to step outside and embrace new challenges. They view new experiences as opportunities. For them the comfort zone is boring and uninteresting.

I myself try to embark on something different each week that pushes me outside of my limits. For example I recently accepted an offer to deliver three presentations in the USA to a completely new audience. It would have been easier to turn the opportunity down, especially when I heard that one of the presentations would have to be delivered at seven to eight o'clock on a Saturday morning. I actually began to list the reasons why I should say no:

1. I will miss a family weekend.
2. The American market may be completely different, and I could flop.
3. I will have jet lag, which will affect my work for several days afterwards.
4. I am going to have to spend more than fourteen hours on a plane.

The positive energy within me, however, came up with several counterarguments encouraging me to go:

1. It is a new group of people whom I have never presented to before.
2. It could therefore open up a new market for me.

3. There are probably ten times more dentists in the USA than in the UK, which could lead to countless more opportunities.
4. It stretches me beyond my comfort zone.
5. If I am a success, then my self-esteem and confidence will grow accordingly.

The other thought that crossed my mind was that I actually had nothing to lose. If I flopped, I would be the only person who would know about it. It would not affect my UK and other international business.

I went to Atlanta and delivered the three presentations. Luckily, there were successes, and I have been invited back.

Self-confidence is not only critical to our performance within the workplace. It is equally essential to creating and maintaining healthy personal relationships. It empowers us, makes us more engaging, and can even inspire. As a consequence of feeling so at ease with ourselves, we become proactive rather than reactive. We are less defensive and can even step back and laugh at ourselves.

Self-confident individuals take a measured approach towards achieving their goals and do so with a real sense of purpose. They have an overriding belief that anything is possible. It doesn't matter where they fit into the chain of command; from apprentice to the managing director, every aspect of their lives improves.

When our levels of self-confidence are at their highest, it is imperative that we no longer allow other people's negativity to filter in. It is vital that we avoid negativity, as it can be like a toxin, damaging our state of well-being.

Think for a moment about your own circle of friends and acquaintances. Are there people within it who are constantly negative? When you ask them how things are, do they spend the next few minutes painting a gloomy picture? You will usually find that these kinds of people will blame others for their own predicaments. They'll point an accusing figure at the government, the NHS, or CQC (Care Quality Commission) before they look at themselves. That kind of negativity can influence our own thinking, if we allow it to do so.

It is vital to distance yourself from negative people and their way of thinking. Your life will be so much better without them. We must try to mix only with those people who share our core beliefs and who encourage and support our visions and dreams.

One excellent method of maintaining your self-confidence is by following up your patients after they've had a challenging procedure. But before I explore this in detail, I want to describe what I do in my business and the advantages that it brings. I make a point of contacting as many clients as possible after they've taken one of my programmes. Every week I make at least ten calls to discover what impact my course has had on their businesses.

This contact has the following benefits:

1. It builds better relationships with my clients, creating an even stronger bond.
2. It is important for me to know that my programme is working.
3. When my dentists tell me what has worked and share stories with me, I can relay these examples to future clients.
4. I can offer further assistance. It is quite normal for one of my clients to have an issue or a challenge, to which I can offer a useful solution or a brand-new strategy.
5. These calls often lead to referrals and future introductions.

Whenever I make these follow-up calls, the clients always seem to appreciate that I've been in contact again. And though that in itself makes calling worthwhile, there is another reason why I do so. If my delegates have benefitted from my courses, it gives an enormous boost to my confidence. It reaffirms that my programme is working, which in turn reassures me that I can continue to quote my prices to future clients.

Additionally these conversations provide me with new success stories which I can then share with delegates on my future courses. Often during follow-up calls my clients tell me of a new way in which they've used my advice. I liken this to my very own 'eureka moment', as there's nothing more refreshing than to learn of an original way in which my work has been adopted for the betterment of a business. It all proves just how beneficial a follow-up conversation can be.

Eighteen years ago two dentists took one of my sales courses, I followed them up by telephone six weeks later, and the rest has been history. I often wonder what might have happened to my life if I had not made those two follow-up telephone calls.

Whenever an orthodontist finally removes a brace on 'debond day', one of his or her greatest fears is surely that the patient will question whether the entire process has been worth it. In an extreme case a patient may even believe that the last twelve months have been a complete waste of time and money. Dentists who've completed a complex cosmetic procedure such as a veneer may occasionally receive a similarly snide remark.

Such occurrences are thankfully very rare. It's much more likely that instead you can reflect upon a catalogue of satisfied customers who've been glowing in their praise of you and equally delighted with the changes you've made to their smiles. There is nothing better than a patient who genuinely feels that you've delivered a life-changing improvement. Moments like this are incredibly uplifting for dentist and patient alike.

If you take the time to follow up with your clients after a significant treatment, it is likely to be of enormous benefit. The conversations will provide you with insight into how your work has affected them, and they can share their experiences of procedures with you. These may include:

1. Increased self-confidence in their personal lives.
2. Stronger belief in their smiles has allowed them to develop new relationships.

3. New levels of self-esteem have improved their results at their jobs.

I suggest that, whenever possible, these findings should be passed on to your team. It can provide them with a similar boost in confidence. It is also likely to encourage them to conduct their own follow-ups, allowing even greater feedback to be shared within your practice. When everyone is pulling in the same direction, it will promote even greater success for your business.

In a race it is not necessarily the team with the fastest athletes who win the relay, but the ones who haven't dropped the baton! It's a principle which doesn't just apply to sport.

To summarise:

1. Like exercise, self-confidence requires a daily workout. This can be achieved by taking on a new challenge outside your regular comfort zone.
2. Following up your patients can also improve your self-confidence. Hearing of ways in which your work has improved the lives of others is a particularly cathartic experience.
3. Rid yourself of any negativity which encompasses you. Avoid the negative people who may otherwise bring you down with them.

Chapter 10

The power of evidence

One method of determining why you should feel comfortable with the prices you charge is by hearing directly from the very mouths you've help to improve! By putting together a portfolio of testimonials from your patients following treatment, you will effectively be assembling the most significant evidence of the quality of your work. There is nothing more convincing for a future patient than for him or her to see real examples of how you've improved other people's teeth at your surgery.

These testimonials may take the form of 'before and after' photographs. They could be written letters sharing details of successful procedures, or perhaps even videos. It is the last two types of testimonial that I will explore in this section of the book. Obtaining this kind of commendation can be extremely advantageous for the entire practice. Letters and videos are particularly compelling tools when it comes to listing the fees for the services you offer.

I personally favour video, as it effectively means that the patient and not the dentist will be doing the selling. It will be a patient's words and not yours that future patients will be hearing. I particularly like videos because it means that happy patients will be explaining the major advantages of your work, while at the same time portraying the emotional benefits too. They will be describing what impact treatment has had on their lives and, in some cases, what they are now able to do that they previously couldn't. It is a very powerful argument.

Shortly I will be explaining the essential ingredients of a successful video and the mechanics of how to collect it. However, first and foremost, there will be certain dentists who'll need convincing of video's value. They will undoubtedly have a list of objections that they believe will prevent them from even trying:

1. Patients won't want to participate.
2. I wouldn't want to do one, so how can I convince them?
3. We would need consent.

At this point, therefore, I need to be at my most persuasive.

A few years ago I read a book by Robert Cialdini, a professor of marketing and psychology at Arizona State University. It's called *Influence: The Psychology of Persuasion*, has sold more than two million copies worldwide, and is widely acclaimed as one of the foremost works on the subject of communication. I strongly suggest that you read this book sometime.

I particular like the story about a jewellery shop that was experiencing poor sales of certain pieces. Once it increased the prices of the items, their sales increased.

One of the key principles in the book is called *reciprocation*, which basically states that when one person does a favour for another, the recipient will feel the need to return the favour. In business terms, if a job of work is completed beyond expectation, then a client will feel obliged to do something back.

Relating this to dentistry, a patient whose cosmetic treatment has transformed his appearance and given him more confidence may well feel so elated that a simple thank you seems insufficient. At this point the suggestion of recording a testimonial video would surely be a formality. While there may be some who feel speaking into a camera would represent their worst nightmares, there are also many who would be happy to oblige. For those who do feel that this is beyond them, I have another suggestion later in this chapter

Once the principle has been agreed, you will then have to secure the patient's permission by way of a written consent form. I have set out a sample copy for you to use. Naturally, feel free to alter the wording as you see fit.

> Dear —,
>
> I would like to request your permission to use a video testimonial and/or your photographs on our website and for marketing purposes. This means third parties would be able to

view the video and/or photographs and listen to or read your words.

If you sign the attached form, it means that you agree to the following:

1. (Practice name here) is permitted to publish your testimonial and/or your photograph as many times as required in the ways mentioned above.

2. (Practice name here) will not use your testimonial or photograph for any purpose other than for the website or for general promotion of the practice's dental services.

3. (Practice name here) will not resell the material to any third parties without your consent.

If you agree to permit the clinic to produce a video testimonial and photographs to be published, please complete this consent form:

Consent

I agree to the shooting of a video testimonial and the taking of photographs for use by (practice name here) to promote the clinic.

I will notify the clinic if I decide to withdraw this consent.

Name of client: _____

Signature of client:_____

Date: _____

The next stage of the process is to set out what you would like the patient to say. He or she will need your guidance. Long before you decide upon the script, I strongly suggest that you discuss the wording with your team. Ask them to identify the most common objections that prevent patients from proceeding with treatment. You will need genuine examples.

After these discussions you may well conclude that price is one of the issues. If so, then imagine how powerful it will be for the patient who is wavering to listen to another who has not only spent the money, but has been thrilled by the results!

I recommend these five questions to form the basis of your video testimonial script:

1. What was your problem before you came to see us?
2. What treatment did you have?
3. What have been the major benefits to you since having the treatment? Please share an example.
4. Was it a good investment of both time and money?
5. What is your advice to people who are considering the treatment?

You can't underestimate the value of capturing on tape the words of a happy patient extolling the virtues of your treatment. A video answering these five questions will undoubtedly overcome any objections.

Equally, watching one of your patients describe his or her overwhelming satisfaction will serve as a welcome boost to all your staff's confidence. It will reaffirm to all concerned that the practice has the ability to improve people's lives.

Once you have filmed these videos, they are extremely easy to upload onto YouTube and, of course, your own website under the heading *Success Stories*. This type of promotion will enable your business to stand out from the competition. It will show other patients the benefits of your work.

While many people seem to be seeking their five minutes of fame, courtesy of the endless stream of reality TV shows, it is also true that many more are not. Consequently you'll find that some of your patients won't take part in a video, no matter how convincing you try to be.

At this point it's worth adopting the findings of another of Robert Cialdini's books, *Influence: Science and Practice*, in which he states that when an initial request is turned down, clients will feel even more obliged to accept a second, lesser request. Consequently, you should find that a testimonial letter is readily obtained from these patients.

Letters can also be powerful marketing tools. They can be used as part of a portfolio album, or perhaps placed strategically around your reception area for perusal by patients as they await their appointments. An apparently random encounter with a well-written letter can be particularly persuasive and may lead to new opportunities for the practice.

Since the start of the credit crunch, people's buying habits have changed, maybe forever. They won't necessarily buy the cheapest product or service, but they certainly want value for money. I strongly believe that people need convincing; you have to work harder for acceptance of your plans. Testimonials, whether videos or letters, form part of the evidence-gathering strategy which I would encourage every business to adopt.

Such a strategy can be started today by the purchase of a basic flip-up camera, which for an investment of around £90 is an ideal way to begin your recordings. With the additional purchase of an attractive photo album for another £30, for little more than a hundred quid you have the beginnings of a new, impactful marketing campaign—one which will pay for itself many times over!

To summarise:

1. People's buying habits have changed. A great deal more time is now spent researching before buying. Evidence is therefore a prerequisite.
2. There are many people who'll be happy to help you—just ask them!
3. Gather all types of evidence: video whenever possible, photographs, and letters. Letters in particular must be kept updated, as ten-year-old letters are much less impactful than recent ones.

Chapter 11

Know your numbers

Almost all of the dentists I have ever coached have reluctantly admitted to being guilty of the following scenario: faced with quoting a price for a treatment, they have mentally started off with a figure of, say, £400, which by the time they've actually uttered the words somehow comes out as just £350! They've found the prospect of talking about money so uncomfortable that they've actually offered a discount without even having been asked for one. In this case, it's a whopping £50—the equivalent of almost 15 per cent.

Those same dentists have also admitted to carrying out basic procedures free of charge because the treatments only take a few minutes to complete.

If either of these situations has a familiar ring, then I strongly advise you to read this chapter several times over. I hope it will irreversibly change your attitude towards charging. In some cases, a new attitude may save your practice from bankruptcy!

Whenever I deliver any of my courses, I am staggered by the number of cases of undercharging that are revealed. At a recent ethical sales course, one of my clients described how he used to knock £30 off each filling. His price sheet listed it at £130 but he would ask for just £100. This represents a substantial 23 per cent reduction which no patient had ever requested! Such a policy means that your patient is getting a discount and doesn't even know about it. If you are going to play that game, at least get credit for it by telling the patient about the discount.

Exploring this one example, we calculated that it cost his practice around £10,000 per year. This particular dentist had only been in business for five years. When I pointed out that he'd already lost £50,000 through this one unnecessary discount, he was stunned. He was ashamed to admit that there were many other treatments for which he would regularly undercharge his patients; by then, however, he was far too embarrassed to admit what they were!

On my programmes I often discuss a concept called 'the 10 per cent rule'. It concerns the harm that a regular discount can do to a business. I ask the question, 'What does a 10 per cent reduction in price do to your margins?' Most dentists believe that it will equate to a 10 per cent reduction in profits, but the reality is much worse.

Here are some examples of this important concept.

For every £100 of sales, assume your costs are £65. That leaves a gross margin of £35. If you were to consistently reduce your prices by 10 per cent, it would mean your sales are now reduced to £90, while your costs remain unchanged. Your gross margin has become £25. In effect, your profits have been reduced by a staggering 29 per cent!

I am certain that most of you have heard the saying, 'Turnover is vanity and profit is sanity'. It does you no little good to get more patients through the door via discounting if each is reducing the profit you make.

Look at another example of rising costs. With the introduction of additional bureaucracy in the UK and a significant rise in business overheads in the last few years, there has been a major impact on dental practices. Using simple figures as before, let's assume that your total sales are £100, while your costs are £65, again leaving a gross margin of £35. Costs then go up to £70, the equivalent of a 7.7 per cent increase. If your prices don't increase to reflect this, then your gross margin will come down from £35 to £30. That equates to a drop of around 15 per cent.

These examples demonstrate very clearly that even a small differential in cost can have a dramatic impact on profit. Many dentists I've spoken to have reacted to the on-going recession by freezing their prices, despite an increase in their overheads. They are fearful that any increase in price would risk losing their patients altogether. Not increasing prices to keep in line with rising costs can in time only lead to bankruptcy.

It is also paramount that the price increase must reflect an equivalent *percentage* rise seen in overheads. For example, if costs go up from £65 to £70 but prices only increase from £100 to £105, it will actually equate to an overall decrease in your margins. The monetary amount—an additional five pounds—is not the same as the percentage of increase. In this example, costs have risen more than 7 per cent, while revenues have gone up only 5 per cent, leading margins to decline to 33 per cent. A price rise therefore must keep in line with the percentage increase in your costs, or your profits will begin to suffer.

In all the above examples I have worked on a 10 per cent increase in costs. Imagine what the figures would be in the case of the dentist who reduced his price per filling by 23 per cent! It's an alarming thought. I asked that dentist if he thought that his patients would have objected to paying £130 rather than the discounted price. He admitted that in almost every case, it wouldn't have made any difference.

The only way to offset any significant decrease in your margins is to attempt to significantly increase the volume of your sales. To illustrate this point, let's use the above example. A unit of treatment is sold for £100 and you sell 100 of them, with costs of £65 and a profit therefore of £35.

Sales: £100 x 100 = £10,000 in sales
Costs: £65 x 100 = £ 6500 in costs
Profit: £35 x 100 = £3500 in profit

Now with a 10 per cent reduction in price:

Sales: £90 x 100 = £9,000 in sales
Costs: £65 x 100 = £6,500 in costs
Profit: £25 x 100 = £2,500 in profit

Now with 140 sales:

Sales: £90 x 140 = £12, 600 in sales
Costs: £65 x 140 = £9,100 in costs
Profit: £25 x 140 = £3,500 in profit

In other words, to achieve the same absolute profit level you had to begin with, you will need to increase your patient turnover by a whopping 40 per cent. That equates to 140 units of treatment rather than 100. To do this effectively, you might need to work 40 per cent more hours, or increase staff, and therefore overhead, by 40 per cent.

Costs will increase, you'll be feeling fatigued, and perhaps the quality of your work will suffer. It is a vicious circle and one which can be very difficult to reverse. Working around the clock, seven days a week, is completely unsustainable. Yet I know of many dentists who are trying to do exactly that, such are the increasing size of their overheads. This is a club to which you definitely don't want membership!

Dentists often tell me that they reduce their prices for certain treatments in response to nearby practices which have done the same. It seems a natural response to the fear of losing patients to a cheaper competitor.

This is an area which I will tackle in greater detail in Chapter 13. I will be providing strategies which you can implement and also will reassure you that higher prices will not alter your production levels. For the moment, though, simply by studying the sample figures above, you'll recognise that reducing prices is ultimately doomed to failure, even if it does keep you in line with local rivals. It's a game in which there are no winners. No one wins the race to the bottom.

So far I have studied the many negative implications of price reduction. I wonder how many of you are now calculating the genuine cost to your business of this flawed business ploy? My advice is not to dwell upon what's happened before, as it is futile to do so. The important thing to do now is to move on. Charge the correct prices which your specialist work merits. I guarantee that your practice's finances will quickly recover.

At this point it's prudent to look at the impact of a price increase. I will shortly do a similar exercise to the one which I did earlier, only this time with a 10% rise rather than a reduction. The good news is that the impact is both significant and immediate. Dentists tell me they are concerned about raising prices, believing that it will lose them a number of their patients. I want to share some thoughts on this matter straight away:

1. I've already pointed out that generally people do not buy on price alone. While it is an issue, it is rarely *the* issue.
2. People hardly ever discuss the price of crowns and fillings in their everyday conversations with others.
3. The patient is investing in you first and foremost, not your prices. Never forget that the patient's relationship with you is paramount. He or she will trust you and have faith in your expertise. Few people would ever invest in someone they didn't like or in whom they had no faith.
4. Even if you were to lose a few patients (and I don't think you will), it will not affect your income as dramatically as you perceive—as the figures below will demonstrate.

Let's assume your price for fillings is £100 and the cost is £80, leaving a profit of £20. Completing ten fillings per day would therefore give you a profit of £200.

Now let's factor in a price increase of 10 per cent.

The fillings are now priced at £110, the costs remain the same at £80, so the profit per filling has increased to £30—a profit increase of 50 per cent. This means that you will now be making £300 profit per day. Working five days a week and forty-five weeks per year, this equates to a staggering £22,500 per year on fillings alone, all of which goes towards your bottom line!

This is what can be achieved with just a 10 per cent increase in the price of fillings. Even a 5 per cent increase would yield a very pleasant £11,000 in additional annual revenue. Even if you only performed seven fillings a day, losing *three patients per day* (an extremely improbable outcome), this 10 per cent increase in price would still generate more profit. Just think of the extra income that would be generated if this modest increase was applied to the prices of your other treatments too.

I hope that all these mathematical equations will finally convince those who've previously reduced their prices that it is now time to reverse this flawed strategy. Charging correct prices will additionally help to promote your self-confidence, as profits will increase and reinvestment in your business can recommence.

I would never advocate being greedy, but I do want to clarify that while many practices are struggling to survive, a simple price increase could turn their fortunes around. Our credit-crunch era has created a feeling of uncertainty which has made dentists feel that a price increase would scare away their patients. This is simply not the case.

What is much more significant is that while your costs are increasing, so must your prices. Doing nothing to redress this imbalance will have far more serious consequences than the loss of a handful of patients.

I don't profess to be a mathematical genius, nor do I believe that I am an economics expert. But as a business owner for many years, I feel well equipped to offer this advice: *you must regularly review your costs and work out what they equate to per hour*. Once you've calculated these figures, I am sure that any tendency to undercharge or carry out work for free will quickly stop.

A colleague and friend of mine, business coach Chris Barrow, is an expert in the field of number crunching, and I can highly recommend his work. I have heard him speak many times on this specific issue, and he offers programmes on this specialist area of business. If you wish to discuss this further, then you can contact him at coachbarrow@me.com.

Practice owners who are reading this book should be considering holding a team meeting to discuss the overheads associated with running the business. I know of a client who held such a meeting and split the team into two, giving them each a different series of costs to the business. One looked at the heating and electricity bills, the other rates and telephone services. Initially he asked them to estimate what they thought each utility cost the practice each day. On revealing the actual cost a little later, the groups' estimates were as much as 30 per cent short of the true costs. The whole staff was astonished by the figures.

In my experience of working with dentists, many are overwhelmed by the numbers, so there's a good chance that the team members will be too. It's highly likely that none will have an awareness of how expensive it is to run a business. They'll have always wrongly assumed that the dentist takes home all the money which is generated.

I think it's vital, therefore, to make your team aware of the size of these costs in order for them to have a greater understanding of the prices that they are charging. Fundamentally it will give them more faith in these prices and give them the confidence to deliver prices to the patients.

To summarise:

1. Understand the serious implications of reducing prices. Remember the impact that just a 10 per cent reduction will have on your profits.
2. Work out exactly what it costs to run your business. Know these figures and work them out on a cost per hour basis.
3. Discuss these costs with your team. It's important that they are aware of the overheads associated with the practice.
4. Don't be tempted to reduce your prices because a local rival has done so. Ultimately this is a game nobody wins!

Chapter 12

How to communicate value

Have you ever received a price objection from one of your patients? It will usually occur when the person presenting the treatment has failed to sell it well enough and has not communicated the benefits or its true value.

This is my definition of an objection: it is a barrier to a sale which results from a failure to give the product or service its most positive slant. The objection is, in effect, a request for more information.

Unless a price objection is overcome, a sale will not proceed. Often when a sales person receives such an objection, he or she will crumble and become defensive. This is an area I have looked at extensively in my earlier book, *Don't Wait for the Tooth Fairy: How to Communicate Effectively and Create the Perfect Patient Journey in your Dental Practice*.

In this section I will be looking at the best ways in which to discuss the price of your treatment with patients. I will make you feel much more comfortable about talking money. With greater self-confidence, you'll prevent these objections from happening.

As I've discussed earlier, it does seem that when it comes to money, dentists and their teams are distinctly uncomfortable. In some extreme cases there appears to be a reluctance to even quote fees to their patients. Here is a simple tip which should assist you in the future: if you're discussing an extensive treatment plan, rather than saying the word *cost*, use the word *investment* instead.

The definition of *the word cost* is 'an amount that has to be paid or spent to buy or obtain something'.

By contrast, here's the definition of *the word investment*: 'something which is worth buying, because it may be profitable or useful in the future'.

There is a significant difference in these two terms. One implies money leaving your pocket for good; the other suggests a return on your money in the future. I would therefore encourage you to use the word *investment* rather than *cost* wherever possible.

From past experience, I know there is sometimes a reluctance to try this, as it feels unnatural to do so. I assure you that in time it will become second nature, and *investment* will feel like a much more appropriate word to use.

Now that you are using the word *investment*, it's time to discuss what's included. Many patients won't know exactly what's involved, and it is essential to make them aware what they're actually getting for their money.

I hear that often when patients are considering crowns, they have an assumption that a crown will simply come out of a nearby drawer and be slotted straight into their mouths. Consequently the £450 price tag seems excessive. If you clarify the details of the investment, they will have a greater understanding of how much work is actually involved.

Let them know about the temporary crown and the bespoke nature of the one that is to be fitted. Explain how a skilled technician will be making it specifically for the unique shape of the patient's mouth and the tooth it is set to replace. Now would also be a good time to mention any twelve-month guarantees which back up the product.

Think of the difference this detail will make in how a patient views the price.

Some useful words and phrases which will help you discuss price include *manufactured, bespoke, handcrafted, skilled technicians*. All will give the patient a feeling of how much work is being done specifically on his behalf.

You might want to suggest that patients go to the technician's laboratory, where they can have a shade analysis done to colour match the crown with the other teeth. This is something I can highly recommend. From my conversations and work with technicians, they enjoy this kind of interest in their work. Patients who've done this have found it very interesting too, as they very rarely see what goes on behind the scenes. It will also serve as another insight as to why the price of a crown is set much higher than a simple filling. Technicians who've attended my courses have applied their newly acquired knowledge when they meet patients, and by doing so have created fresh opportunities for the dentists.

Here's another example. Imagine quoting a price for orthodontic treatment: 'Your investment for your orthodontic treatment is going to be £3,500. Included in the price is your bespoke brace, which is manufactured by a skilled technician. The fitting and subsequent appointments will all be covered, which could be as many ten visits in the next twelve months. On removing the brace, which we call "debonding", we will fit a retainer which will help preserve your newly straightened teeth. We will then monitor you for a further eighteen months and thereby ensure you will have beautiful, straight teeth for the rest of your life. We are effectively embarking on a two and a half year project together, which is all included in the price.'

Now you can begin to see the value you're creating.

Incidentally, by mentioning the retainers, you are adding another excellent selling point, which I find a number of practices still neglect to mention. There is no logical reason for this omission. By talking in terms of it being two and a half years, you are building a long-term relationship with your patient. You are also showing a degree of care beyond simply fitting the brace.

This kind of information should be included on your website too. Many potential clients shop around on the Internet before planning their visits. They won't just be looking for the cheapest price but the practice which best meets their needs. Attention to detail could tip the balance in your favour.

Even if other practices undertake this, there is a good chance they don't communicate this to the patient. They will often take it for granted that the patient knows this. This is another communication mistake made by dental practices.

I strongly suggest that you look at other treatments you offer and see if you can adopt similar communication tactics.

When quoting price, you must always ensure that you do it with confidence. It is imperative that you don't sound apologetic in any way. When observing a practice during my research, I've actually heard a dental team utter the words, 'I am really sorry to say it's going to be . . . ' Or worse still, 'I hope you're sitting down!' Statements like these sound as though you have little confidence in your own price structure. They merely serve to create doubt in the mind of a patient. Negative language will, by definition, have the potential to lead to a negative response. If you have team members who are prone to this problem, then ensure they read this section of the book.

On my programmes I often use a phrase which refers to the closing stages of a deal. I call it a *test close*. It's basically a question aimed at the patient to ensure that he or she is happy with what you have said about the treatment. Examples include:

'How does that sound?'

'Is that okay?'

These simple questions are invaluable. A positive response from your patient at this point will indicate to you that everything is satisfactory and you can move forward to the acceptance stage of your treatment plan.

This book examines the psychology of the concerns which surround money. It deals with every aspect of this core issue, so you can feel comfortable when charging fees and subsequently ensure that you are running a successful and productive practice.

If you wish to increase the uptake of your treatment plans still further, then you'll need to develop your ethical sales and communication skills. To that end I recommend my earlier book *Don't Wait for the Tooth Fairy*. I also run an extremely successful two-day 'Ethical Sales and Communication' programme. Several thousand dental professionals worldwide have already taken it and continue to reap the rewards for their investment in it.

To summarise:

- When you quote prices, use the word *fees* or, if it is a substantial treatment plan, the word *investment*. Avoid using the word *cost* altogether.
- Provide detailed information about the treatment so that your patient knows exactly what value he or she is getting for the money. It is essential that you proactively create value. Don't make any assumptions about what the patient knows or understands.

- Avoid talking too technically and keep the language simple. Your patients will not understand many of the dental terms you may take for granted.
- Be confident about your prices and never apologise for them. Negative language will lead to negative responses.

Chapter 13

How to sell at a higher price when it is cheaper down the road

The most common questions I'm asked by dentists concern how to stand out from the competition and how to compete on price against other practices in the local area. This is becoming an increasingly difficult challenge, as many patients will shop around before deciding where to go for their treatments. I have heard of potential clients whose desire to have their teeth straightened has led them to conduct a detailed search in which they've compared the services, décor, and pricing of almost every surgery in their cities.

It's worth remembering that what patients can't compare is the standard of the dentistry that they are likely to receive. This is unlike the purchase of a TV, car, or dress, for which you can easily play off one product against another.

That said, there is an argument to suggest that certain treatments are now becoming more commoditised. Orthodontic and implant treatments, for example, are increasingly competitive. In my opinion this is not good for the dental industry, as some practices are championing their prices, using advertisements and social media to steal a march on their competitors. Such tactics take these highly specialised services, with all their many facets, solely down to a price comparison exercise.

I've alluded to the fact that patients will be judging your customer service, waiting room décor, and website. But above all they'll be judging the quality of work by their chosen dentist. Whatever else they may have been impressed by to reach this point, they are ultimately buying you and the expertise you have to offer. Only misguided people will buy dentistry based solely on price. In truth, would you want a patient who'd only come to you because you were the cheapest?

In my experience working across many industries, I've discovered that almost without exception, price buyers are much more trouble than they are worth. They will constantly be looking for cheaper services and are highly unlikely to remain loyal. I also believe that only a tiny minority base their decisions solely on price, whether buying dentistry or anything else. There are much more important factors when it comes to health, such as a personal relationship with the dentist and trust in the dentist's work.

If your local competitors do indulge in advertising their prices, then my advice is simply not to become embroiled in a price war. In Chapter 11 I described in detail how there are no winners when it comes to this battle. Your focus must remain on the quality of service you can provide. Use this to distinguish yourself from your rivals.

Here is an example which highlights the way in which a patient thinks before choosing one dentist over another. While I was in the process of writing this book I was having my hair cut when I noticed that my hairdresser was wearing invisible braces. As I work so closely with the dental profession, I was curious as to why she had them.

A woman in her late twenties, she'd always been unhappy with her top teeth and had been thinking of having them straightened for several years. On seeing several of her clients have similar problems corrected, she decided to do so herself. It appears that this treatment has now become more fashionable.

On further investigation, she revealed that she'd been to six different practices before she made her final choice. Her decision-making process is both fascinating and illuminating.

Here are some of the significant factors which influenced her decision:

1.   Three of the dentists attempted to sell her veneers. She ruled them out immediately.
2.   Two of them built very little rapport with her and made her feel like a number.
3.   Some had spoken too technically, and she was flummoxed by their explanations.
4.   On almost all the visits she was told to go away and think about alternative solutions. However, she'd already decided she wanted invisible braces.

It was only the last dentist who took the time to listen to her needs and understood exactly what she craved. He also said he was in a position to fit her into his schedule almost straight away. He was enthusiastic about the procedure and seemed genuinely excited about the results he would be able to achieve for her. She immediately felt she had confidence in him and made a follow-up appointment before she left the surgery.

This is a classic example in which a patient entered the practice with a problem and left in the knowledge that something was going to be done about it.

Here is another real example of how to get it right. It comes from a Bournemouth-based dentist, Simon Belford, who took four separate programmes with me in a twelve-month period. He has allowed me to use this story for my book.

Here is the tale in his own words:

> A potential new patient contacted me via the 'dentists4implants' website and was interested in replacing a missing upper molar that had recently been extracted by his NHS dentist.
>
> The website enquiry is automatically forwarded to my personal email account. It arrived on a Saturday evening around eight o'clock. I responded immediately, assuring him that we could help him and that I would call him first thing on Monday morning when I had the diary in front of me.

He himself responded that evening and was genuinely impressed that his enquiry had been acknowledged so promptly. He used his business email, which included details of the business that he was in.

I had some spare time on Sunday evening and decided to google his business. I found that he ran management training and public-speaking courses for the local business area.

He'd posted some YouTube videos that I watched and found *genuinely* interesting. When we came to meet for the consultation, I spent a great deal of time talking about his business. I complimented him on the content of his public-speaking video, as I had just recently done a similar course in London.

We built excellent rapport and then moved on to his missing upper molar. He had another molar missing on the left-hand side, but this had been taken out many years ago. The upper lateral incisor was decoronated, but he was seeing his NHS dentist to have this tooth root-filled and then post-crowned. I also found out that he was not happy with the overall colour of his teeth.

We talked about the long-term prognosis of a post crown, how long the procedure would take, and the benefits to him of replacing his front tooth, in terms of his training courses and being in front of groups of people every day. I expanded on this by describing the whitening procedures available and, of course, the 'benefits of the benefits' that he would gain.

Finally, after giving him a rough indication of costs, I informed him that we had time to schedule this procedure for the following week, which would address the issue of the missing front tooth immediately. How would he like to proceed?

The patient was delighted that we could help him. From an Internet enquiry for a single implant, the patient ultimately signed up for:

—Two implant-supported molar crowns (one with GBR)
—One immediately loaded implant to replace the broken incisor
—Two large composite fillings
—One course of tooth whitening

A total of £7,600 largely due to up-sale from the original enquiry!

So what did I do differently?

1. I contacted him promptly and delivered on my promise to organise an appointment.
2. I showed *genuine* interest in him and what he did for a living.
3. I built good rapport.

4. I found out what his concerns were, before trying to sell him *just* what he had originally enquired about, or what I thought he wanted.

5. I asked him 'How does that sound?' and 'Would you like to proceed?'

He never once questioned my fees, and he paid me £3,700 on the first appointment.

Do you think that I will ask him for a testimonial about his implant journey and the care we delivered? Do you think I will say at the end of the treatment, 'What a pleasure it has been treating you. If you have any family or friends who you think would benefit from the services we provide, would you please give them this card?'

This is a perfect example of what is required to win over a new client. Here are some other observations which I would like to highlight:

1. The speed with which Simon contacted the patient was pivotal. How many practices respond that quickly to an enquiry? Communication is becoming more immediate, especially with the onset of smartphones. It is important that we return patient enquiries as quickly as possible. It will pleasantly surprise and impress them.

2. How many other dentists would have demonstrated such diligence by taking the trouble to look up what the potential patient did for

a living and even visiting his website? I would imagine there are very few. Simon's preparation for that first appointment was exemplary.

3. The time that Simon spent building up a rapport was crucial. By finding out what the patient was looking for and then sharing his enthusiasm for the potential results, Simon was able to secure the business without hesitation.

While these may seem simple ideas and largely based on common sense, it still amazes me how few people carry them out. It is one of the best ways of standing out from the competition. Working on the way in which you present yourself can make an enormous difference, and these same principles should also apply to your team.

Some of the patients who visit your surgery, particularly those who have cosmetic work, could be undergoing life-transforming treatment. Their appearances might be affecting their self-confidence, their performance at work, and even their capacity to socialise. These are serious issues. If you want to win their trust and ultimately their business, then you need to display these life-changing qualities every minute of every day that you're at work. These principles of course also apply to your team.

During my presentations I often refer to an experience which has had a major impact on my everyday performance. I went to see the musical *Billy Elliott* at a theatre in London. The show was excellent and the acting so outstanding that the audience felt compelled to respond with a standing ovation at the end. The actors' passion, enthusiasm, and energy had clearly captivated us all.

The show had been running in the West End for many years, largely with the same cast and crew, and naturally the story hadn't altered in all that time. Yet we felt this particular performance had been delivered as if it were opening night. Despite the seemingly repetitive nature of their work, the actors clearly understood the significance of performing to their maximum night after night. The fact that the play continues to play to packed houses is testament to their efforts.

This realisation made me think of the importance of enthusiasm and energy in my own delivery. I always strive to put on a performance as if it were my opening night too. I admit that there are times when I feel tired or distracted by outside occurrences, but I never forget that my clients deserve my very best—not excuses! I am always conscious of the fact that many have travelled long distances, taken time off work, and even shut their practices in order to attend my courses and presentations.

Another factor I bear in mind is that each day I'm at work can potentially lead to more opportunities. At the time of writing this book, I am preparing to deliver a course to four delegates who are travelling from the USA to Manchester especially to take my two-day 'Ethical Sales and Communication' module. On the same programme I also have dentists who are travelling from Paris and Ireland. Thankfully, this is happening more often. I have many clients who come over from Europe, all of whom could open up completely new markets for my business. I am always aware of this when I deliver my programmes.

However hard you try, though, there will still be occasions when you'll need to explain to your clients why you are more expensive than your competitors and why your practice is different to the rest.

Here are a few ways in which you can do this successfully.

Firstly you need to embark on a little homework. Find out if other practices are using the same products and whether they have the same range of services. It is possible that they may not be able to match your range. In many cases, though, a rival is offering only what appears to be a lower price for a treatment. In reality, by the time they've factored in some basic treatment elements priced as 'extras', their final cost will actually work out considerably higher.

Secondly, having conducted this type of research both locally and even nationally, you can begin to work on your specific packages. It's at this point that you will understand your own USP, which stands for 'unique selling point'.

Here's the definition of a USP: 'The factor or consideration presented by a seller as the reason that one product or service is different from and better than that of the competition.

Presenting an effective USP requires a great deal of creativity and imagination. It can only be achieved by putting yourself in your patients' shoes. All too often, dentists become fixated with a product or service while forgetting that it's the patients' needs, not their own, that they must satisfy. It is imperative that you try to be objective and truly scrutinise your range of services.

In Chapter 2 I described the turkey farm in Berkshire which sells some of its turkeys at £150 per bird. This is some fifteen times more expensive than the average supermarket turkey. Despite the extraordinary price tag, the farm is extremely successful. On its website, the managers explain in detail why the turkeys are so highly priced:

- Reared in spacious open barns, cheery orchards and grass meadows. Free range turkeys are outside every day from 6 weeks old.
- Natural balanced cereal diet. Rich in Oats. No animal protein or growth promoting additives. Free range birds also eat natural vegetation, including grass & wild herbs.
- Fully mature adult birds, 6 to 7 months old in all weight categories. This provides a dense meat & natural fat layer to ensure a succulent texture when cooked
- Prepared on the farm premises with minimum stress to the birds. Dry plucked by hand. Game-hung for 2 weeks. Simply refrigerated for Christmas Day—no heavy chilling. 100% pure turkey.
- Each turkey carries our quality guarantee, which includes a money-back commitment in the unlikely event of dissatisfaction.

This is effectively an impressive list of USPs.

I am sometimes challenged to explain why my courses are different to those of my rivals and how I am able to achieve such impressive results. I often use the following explanation:

Dear Mr Client,

We do not lecture on our programmes, but we coach our delegates. I liken it to learning how to drive a car. We provide the techniques, materials, and theory before demonstrating how they are applied to real-life situations in your business.

Under my guidance, you will have an opportunity to practice what you've learned. I will ensure that you are developing these new skills effectively. In this way you will be building your self-confidence, allowing you to use these new methods successfully and ensuring that they become something you can use automatically when you return to your practice.

With this new skill set, you will increase your ratio of treatment plan acceptance significantly.

I guarantee that you won't just know what to do but also how to do it. My programmes are hands-on, fun, and inspirational.

I can give this explanation at any time of the day or night. If you wake me up at three in the morning and ask me, I will give you the same answer. You and your team need to be equally word perfect. On-going training and coaching are essential.

So what can we learn from the turkey seller and the business coach alike that can also be applied to dentistry? It's all in the USPs. Think deeply about what makes you unique. Look at the other practices and realise why you are so much better than the rest.

There are a number of different ways in which you can emphasise your standout qualities. They include:

- How the treatment is delivered.

- What your proposition includes (i.e. the package).

- The experience of the dentist: his or her credentials and particular areas of expertise. (Please do not be afraid to sell the credentials of the dentist. I can promise you, your competitors will not be.)

- The quality of your aftercare.

- The high standards of your customer service.

- The hours you are open and flexibility of appointment.

To assist you in determining your USPs, I will refer to the specific example of teeth straightening. This is becoming one of the most popular treatments for patients, particularly following the advent of invisible braces. As it has become more commoditised, so it has become even more important for each practice to emphasise what makes its service different.

When I'm coaching, I instruct my delegates to elaborate on their aftercare policies and in particular to make reference to what happens after the braces come off. I think it's essential to describe the use of retainers and the subsequent eighteen months of observation which you undertake to ensure that the teeth remain perfect. I believe that these are all USPs, and in an era of non-existent aftercare, this is an exception of which to be very proud.

Another example of your proposition is that you could also include teeth whitening free of charge in your price, while making sure to highlight that it has a £395 value. This works for the following reasons:

1. Teeth whitening is not particularly expensive for you to include and yet is of tremendous value to the patient.
2. Everyone craves whiter teeth.
3. You will achieve better results for your patients and the 'before and after' pictures will look that much more striking. Such images can only serve to encourage further patients to invest in the process. It is great for marketing and promotion on your website.

By adopting these example strategies, you will have simply and impressively described the after care a patient will receive and even added teeth whitening to the package. your USPs will have begun to emerge.

Promoting this package on your website must be your next priority in order to publicise what you have to offer. Finally, your reception team must be fully briefed so that they are aware of all the benefits that you have available and can relay the necessary information to prospective clients.

Now, even if your competitors are offering a similar package, it is highly unlikely that they will also have undertaken the hours of preparation time required to convey this successfully to their patients. Added to that, you will have an attractive and succinct website to promote your products. All these things together will truly make you stand out from the crowd.

I must emphasise one very important point. In a previous chapter, I mentioned that it is very unprofessional to criticise the National Health Service; the same rule applies to competitors. When you communicate your USPs, you must never criticise other dental practices. It is very unprofessional. If a patient is querying why he should come to you as opposed to another practice, a clear explanation of your USPs and what you can deliver that is different should suffice.

I want to leave you with one very important message and reinforce some lessons I have already discussed. Recently, I was coaching a client who was taking one of my 'High Impact Presentation' courses, and he mentioned that he was not having success with the presentations he was giving.

After a lot of questioning on my part, he confessed that he was bored giving the same talk, which he gave at least once a month. That is why he was not achieving the success he felt he deserved. It wasn't the presentation and the content that were boring; it was just the speaker who was bored giving it.

This is a shame. Day in and day out, yes, we give the same presentations; yes, we communicate the same messages. But always remember that the person you deliver it to is probably hearing it for the first time. Always have that in the back of your mind. It's show time all the time. Let's perform like it's the first night.

To summarise:

- The best way to stand out from the crowd is to be you. Work on you and your team.
- Create your unique USP(s) and ensure your team can communicate that.
- Don't take anything for granted when you are communicating to your patients. Tell them the story. It might be the first time they have heard it.

In 1998 two dentists took part on Ashley's 'Ethical Sales and Communication' programme. They took part with delegates from all industries, from all walks of life. Ashley followed them both up by telephone six weeks later and he soon discovered that the programme had changed their lives. They told him that they felt more comfortable communicating the benefits of dental treatment, talking fees and both admitted for the first time, they were both delivering the Dentistry they loved doing and that the patients wanted.

They were both so delighted with the programme, that they introduced the course to their friends and colleagues and six months later, Ashley delivered his first ever Ethical Sales & Communication Programme to the Dental Market. Since then, over 7000 dental delegates have taken this programme in the UK and now all over the world. This programme is legendary in the UK dental world and is probably one of the most sought after programmes in dentistry today.

In addition to the **Ethical Sales and Communication Programme**, Ashley and his team deliver revolutionary thinking and life-changing strategies for subjects such as **World Class Patient Journey, High Impact Presentation Skills, Creating a High Performance Team,** and

Reception—How to Turn Telephone Enquiries into Appointments.

Ashley also works with a very forward group of dentists and orthodontists who comprise the **Serious Players Club**, an entrepreneur group. He has delivered over 23,000 hours of workshops, training courses, and presentations to the dental market.

Ashley is the author of ***Helping Patients to Say YES*** and ***Don't Wait for the Tooth Fairy: How to Communicate Effectively and Create the Perfect Patient Journey.*** He has also contributed to the ***Dental Masters*** series.

Simply put, he is the best at getting dentists and their teams to communicate with their patients, which results in world-class patient journeys, the creation of more opportunities, more patients saying yes to treatment plans, and increased profits for practices.

Ashley has lived in Manchester, England all his life and lives with his wife, Graziella, and two daughters, Enrica and Martina. When he is not working, he enjoys days out with the family in the countryside, walking, running, boxing, and watching his beloved Manchester United.

Ashley writes an email newsletter which is read by over 15,000 dentists worldwide. It is full of useful tips and ideas to make you more successful. To receive this free of charge, please visit **www.ashleylatter.com** to sign up.

There you can also visit the Learning Zone, which is full of hundreds of free articles and videos.

Ashley is available to deliver presentations at your conferences, please email ashley@thesellingcoach.com or call the office on **(0044) (0)161 724 8728**.